The Debt Forgiveness Book

How to Negotiate with Creditors, Especially Credit Card Companies & the IRS

Debt: $18,187.44
Settled for: $3,700

Debt: $27,077.37
Settled for: $8,123.22

I0040507

Debt: $18,129.46
Settled for: $2,000

Debt: $10,362.00
Settled for: $3,040

Debt: $8,789.90
Settled for: $4,598

Debt: $16,608.79
Settled for: $2,000

Brian Lacher

The Debt Forgiveness Book

How to Negotiate with Creditors, Especially Credit Card Companies & the IRS

by

Brian Lacher

Debt: $18,187.44
Settled for: $3,700

Debt: $27,077.37
Settled for: $8,123.22

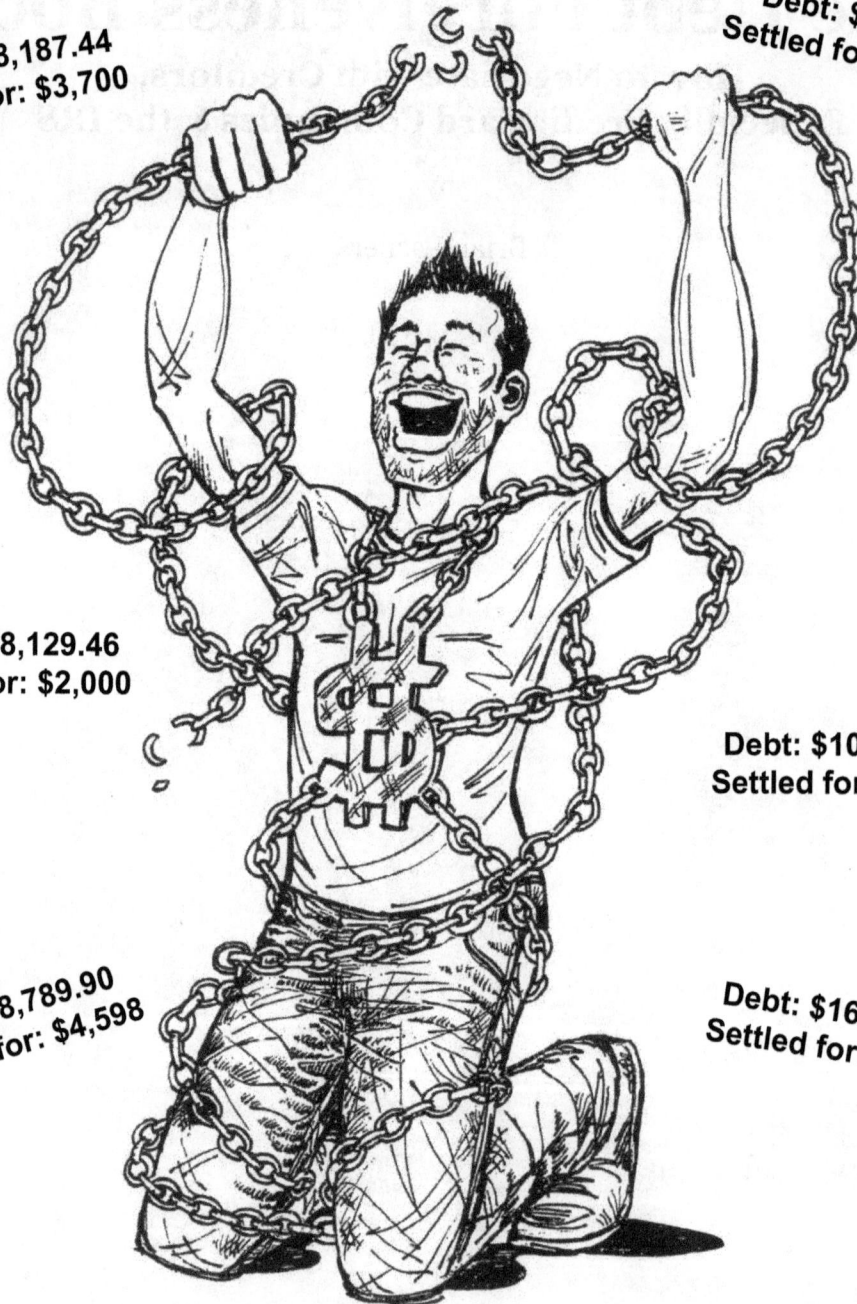

Debt: $18,129.46
Settled for: $2,000

Debt: $10,362.00
Settled for: $3,040

Debt: $8,789.90
Settled for: $4,598

Debt: $16,608.79
Settled for: $2,000

ISBN: 978-0-9966177-7-2

Print Edition #2

www.findingfreedomfromdebt.com

Contents

Contents

Introduction

It was a credit card nightmare! With over $150,000 in unsecured credit card debt, back tax payments due to the IRA. Creditors calling relentlessly wanting some sort of payment. I lost 75% of my income in a short period of time. Had a house payment, utilities, seven children to provide for. I had never missed a payment before, but now I couldn't make the payments, keep food on the table, and a roof over my family's head. What could I do? Where should I turn? Is there any way I could get out of this reality of living nightmare? I'm about to share how I survived negotiating with credit card companies.

I wrote this book to help others through the process of negotiating and settling with credit card companies without filing bankruptcy. I want to share the mistakes I made to keep others from doing the same and I want to give readers hope that things will be all right. It's not the end of the world. Life is truly worth living. Also, for people going through this struggle, I want to be an encouragement so that they may rise above the fear of the overwhelming debt. With the weight of debt and trying to provide for the household, there is an overwhelming feeling to give up or quit. I know how you may be feeling right now, but there is hope.

Let me repeat: There is hope! Don't make the same mistakes I did. This book will teach you <u>how to approach the credit card companies if you don't want to file bankruptcy.</u> This book will also show you the results I have achieved, as well as truth and lies the credit card companies will tell you. Also, I will warn you about what to accept and what not to accept from the credit card companies as settlements, and help you with that process. The final chapter is very important. People have asked me how I got through this nightmare. Therefore, I wrote a whole chapter called *Getting Through It* to answer that question. I encourage you to read through the complete chapter because it can give you the greatest comfort and hope needed to get through this struggle.

As you read this book, there are many places that I will repeat myself. The reason for repeating the subject is so that the important information is covered. I have put a number of illustrations in the appendix chapter to be referenced. You will see some of the actual correspondence my lawyer and I had with credit card companies. Be sure to take a look at them so that you can get an idea of what you may receive from a credit card company. Also, some readers may only read one chapter. If that is the case, I want to make sure that they have all the important information that goes with the subject of the chapter. Bear with me if there are areas that may seem to be repeating; it is for a reason. I want to make certain that valuable information is included in every place it is relevant.

The day my wife and I "drew a line in the sand" by saying no more living off of credit cards I had a lot of questions, wondering what will happen next. *Give me the worst case scenario. Will the creditors work with me? Will they try to take my house away? Will I have to move my family to a different location? Will I be put in jail?* There were just a lot of questions going through my mind.

I went to the internet to look for helpful information, but I couldn't find anything. Since

I documented everything as I went through the process of negotiating with creditors, I decided to document my journey in book form to help you and others learn how to negotiate with credit card companies and creditors.

As I dealt with the credit card companies and creditors, many times I was able to settle for pennies on the dollar! Of course, I cannot guarantee the results will be the same for you and your situation. The principles in this book will help prepare you to deal with the credit card companies. My hope is that you don't make the same mistakes I did, and that you will find HOPE in the midst of this process.

There is HOPE!

How bad was it?

HERE IS A QUICK OVERVIEW:

- 10 major credit cards with over $150,000 of unsecured debt
- 6 gas cards with balances due
- 2 department stores with over $2,000 due
- IRS back taxes due because of non-payment and late fees
- Business Vendors, owed money to parts suppliers
- Everyday expenses of food, shelter, utilities, etc., for a family of nine
- Lack of income, couldn't pay the bills, I couldn't refinance my house.

Here are some <u>actual examples</u> of negotiating with the credit card companies:

1. Debt of $18,187.44 with Card Company A   settled for $3,700
2. Debt of $16,608.79 with Card Company B   settled for $2,000
3. Debt of $18,129.46 with Card Company C   settled for $2,000
4. Debt of $27,077.37 with Card Company D   settled for $8,123.22
5. Debt of $10,362.00 with Card Company E   settled for $3,040
6. Debt of $19,343.59 with Card Company F   settled for $10,000
7. Debt of $8,789.90 with Card Company G   settled for $4,598
8. Debt of $20,967.00 with Card Company H   settled for $13,000
9. Debt of $1,077.57 with Card Company I   settled for $550

One more credit card company, this one took me to court:

10. Debt of $12,398.88 with Card Company J   settled for $12,398.88+interest

So I paid the full amount plus interest, over a 4 year period.

If you add up just these 10 cards, **total debt was $152,942.00**

I settled for $59,409.22 *(plus interest for card company J)*

As I prepared to draw a line in the sand and not pay the credit card companies, not because I didn't want to, but because I wasn't able to, I had many questions. Some of my questions were:

- What will happen next if I don't pay the credit card bills?
- What arrangements should I make or what should I not do?
- Who can I turn to? Can I trust anybody?
- Will the credit card companies work with me, or do I need to file bankruptcy?
- Even if I could make arrangements, where will I get the money?
- Will I be taken to court? If so, what do I need to do?
- Will they take the house?

The rest of this book will answer those questions and more. Many of you may have the same questions, wondering what will happen to you and your family.

NOTE: I must add this disclaimer: I am only able to share with you my experience of negotiating with the creditors. I cannot guarantee or suggest that you will get the same results. The samples in this book are copies of the actual letters sent and received by me or my lawyer. I have blocked out the names for privacy purposes. Some of the letters came by fax, therefore the quality may not be the best, but you will be able to see the intent of the letter.

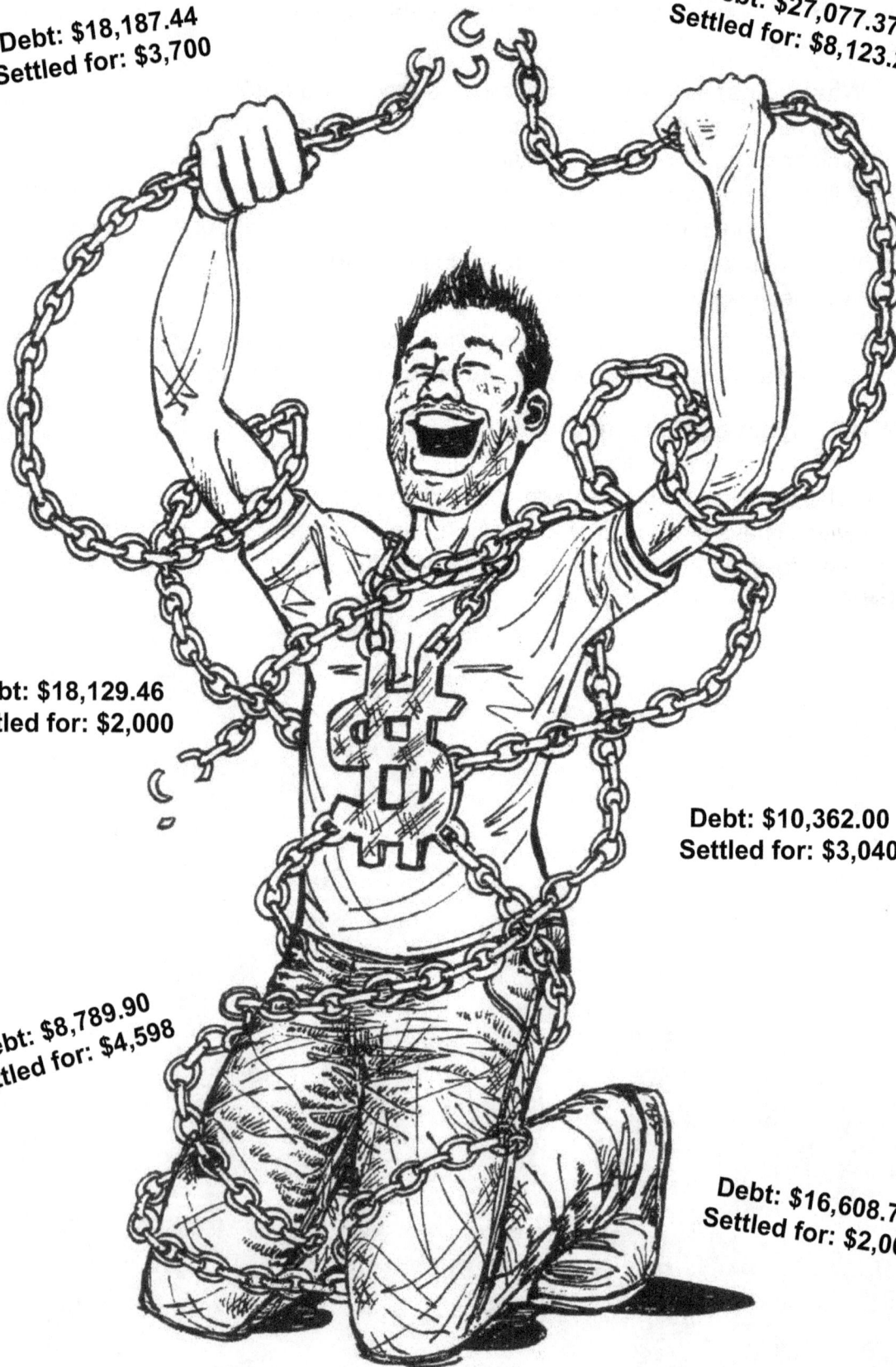

Debt: $18,187.44
Settled for: $3,700

Debt: $27,077.37
Settled for: $8,123.22

Debt: $18,129.46
Settled for: $2,000

Debt: $10,362.00
Settled for: $3,040

Debt: $8,789.90
Settled for: $4,598

Debt: $16,608.79
Settled for: $2,000

1. My Story

What happened?

The problem of being in debt didn't happen overnight. In fact, it took a number of years. I was sinking deeper into debt every day. It was so bad that every day I woke up and went to work knowing I would be further in debt at the end of the day than I was at the beginning. This was repeated day after day after day after day, month after month after month, year after year. It went on for years. Owning my own business, the "American Dream," I thought things would turn around, that it would get better, but it didn't. I had one employee and I was able to keep him paid, but was not able to pay the withholding taxes on time. This created a problem with the IRS. A number of quarters would go unpaid, causing penalties and interest that only caused the debt to grow. Something had to change.

Cash was so tight that if I sold a product, I would buy the item on credit hoping to pay it off when the customer would pay (sometimes thirty to sixty days later). Meanwhile other expenses would arise, like making a house payment, putting food on the table for a family of nine, keeping gas in the vehicles, keeping the insurance paid, etc. So the money didn't go toward paying off the item that I purchased for the customer. It went to cover everyday expenses. The credit card companies would increase their rates, causing me to pay higher interest. Towards the end, I had accumulated over $150,000 in unsecured credit card debt.

I put the business up for sale, thinking if the business sold it would clear most of the debt. The idea was good in theory. In fact, I had a third party appraise the business. My main problem was finding a buyer that would pay the full asking price in one lump sum.

After many months somebody finally bought the business but paid almost a third of the appraised value and purchased it on land contract with only a small down payment.

That changed my plan of paying on the credit cards to lower the balances. It was important though to sell the business even at a loss so I wouldn't be going further into debt. Selling the business would eliminate the monthly overhead that weighed me down. It freed me to find another job so I could add to the monthly payments that I received from selling the business.

Mile Marker… October 2008

There are occasions when you use certain dates as mile markers. It was my wife's birthday and we couldn't afford to go out and celebrate, but some friends gave us a gift card to a local restaurant. We decided to go out to eat. It had been a long time because the money wasn't available to justify eating out. While at the restaurant, my wife and I had the conversation that the future didn't look good down the current path on we were on. (Good communication with your spouse is important.) We decided no more credit cards from here on. Any item we bought would be with cash only. This was not an easy decision because we had been living off credit cards for so long. We used that birthday date to draw a line in the sand. Things were going to get tough, really tough. Did I say tough? They would get *really* tough. It was at the same time that the economy was in a tailspin with a downward spiral. Businesses were either laying off or closing their doors. The unemployment rate in our area was reaching 19%. The sales for my business were drying up, dropping by 75%. The overhead, the cost of rent, the utilities, the insurance cost, the house payment, etc. was still the same, but the cash flow was vanishing. This mile marker occurred four months before we sold the business.

My wife and I tried to refinance our house. We had over 50% equity in it. The problem was, the banks were not loaning money and the financial credit crunch was in full force at this time. The only thing left to do was to not pay on the credit cards and only pay the primary bills like the groceries, electric, water, gas, and make minimum payments on the gas cards. We scaled back even more than before. Going into winter, we cut back by turning down the heat, bought only a few Christmas gifts, and bought only necessities. With a lack of income and huge overhead expenses, we were not able to pay the bills. I asked the question, "What next?" For the last thirty years we had always committed to making our payments on time, but now that had changed. What will happen if we don't pay our bills?

The first month of not paying the credit cards wasn't too bad because the credit card companies thought we just forgot to pay them. So they slapped on a late fee and sent another statement the next month. The following month the creditors started to call. They were asking for payment. Because I had nine major credit cards, we receive a lot of phone calls. The creditors wanted payment, but we didn't have the money. *What will I do? What will I tell the creditors? Will they work with me? What will happen? Will they take away my house? Will they take away my cars although they were paid off? Will they garnish my wages? What is going to happen?*

The rest of this book will help explain what happened, the things that I did wrong, the things I did right, how I worked with the credit card companies and how you can too.

Good News:

The good news is that the United States doesn't have a debtor's prison for those that file bankruptcy. My intention was not to file bankruptcy but I did have to consider it as an option a few times. In fact, I went to a lawyer to discuss the possibilities. He strongly suggested that I file bankruptcy but I didn't want to. I also had a banker tell me that I would be better off to file bankruptcy. I knew that if I did, it would be on my credit record for at least seven years. Although I had thirty years of great credit and hadn't missed any payments, things were changing. My business was failing, the money was getting tighter, and the bills were getting harder to pay.

Although my credit rating was important, it wasn't the biggest concern. I knew that the credit rating would affect the car insurance cost, along with other costs. But I couldn't be concerned about the credit rating; I would just need to rebuild it at a later time. For now my credit rating was going to be destroyed.

At this time I was operating on a cash basis, but I still wanted out of this debt. There-for, I needed to settle with each card company, if possible. If not, I would be forced to file bankruptcy. It would have been quicker and maybe easier. I would have had more cash to live on, but still, I wanted to try and settle with each company. The first ones that were willing to work with me received money from items that I sold. The other creditors had to go on a payment plan. The following chapters will explain much of those details.

As I close out this chapter I want to share some of the ways the stress of debt was affecting me as a person. I found myself having trouble thinking clearly and had difficulty processing my thoughts. It was getting so bad that I had trouble speaking. I became more reserved in what I said and how I would say it. I had trouble sleeping. If I did get to sleep I had trouble getting out of bed the next morning. I didn't want to face another day because I was going further into debt each day I awoke. When I did get out of bed, I had trouble leaving the house; I didn't want to face people and have to answer any questions like, "how's life going?" If I did leave the house, I didn't want to come home because I knew there would be creditors that I would need to call back and deal with. Plus, coming home would mean going to bed soon, then waking up again to be further in debt. What a terrible cycle, day-after-day-after-day. I will say there was something that turned that whole cycle around. I will mention it in detail in the final chapter of *Getting Through It*. That is one chapter you won't want to skip.

2. Mistakes I Made

Don't make the same mistakes that I did.

I had a friend that would say to me, "Whatever you do, don't make the same mistake I did."

I would ask, "What was that?"

He said, "I married too young."

"How old were you when you got married?" I would ask.

He replied, "I was 40 years old."

We would laugh at that but his words of 'don't make the same mistake I did' hit me. I don't want to repeat somebody else's mistakes; I want to learn from them. If somebody has already been down that path and there could have been a better outcome, then I want to know about it; I want to learn from it.

Therefore, I say to you, don't make the same mistakes I did. Let me list a few of them for you:

1. Didn't buy a phone recorder soon enough
2. Didn't talk to the creditors on my terms
3. Didn't leave money in savings long enough
4. Didn't stagger payments
5. Didn't sell excess items soon enough
6. Didn't communicate when needed
7. Told my lawyer I had a large down payment available
8. Didn't pay the IRS First

Allow me to go through these steps in greater detail.

1. <u>Didn't buy a phone recorder soon enough:</u> Eventually I did get one and it was very helpful. I was able to use it to replay conversations so I could get the details. It is very critical to have one. You can either purchase a new digital recorder or download an app on your phone that will record calls. You will be able to play back the conversation to prove the arrangements that were agreed on. Also, the phone recorder may be used as evidence in a court of law if the settlement ever went that far.

When talking to a creditor, at the beginning of the phone conversation, the calling party will say that this phone call is being recorded. You can agree to that and at the same time you can say, "I am recording this conversation also."

During the conversation I would repeat to the representative what needed to be done. That way we understood each other and so the final agreement was recorded. After the phone call, I would write the details of the conversation—what was said and what actions needed to be taken. Record the date, time, who you spoke with, final appointments, payment plan, and length of the call.

See examples for the notes taken in *Appendix Pages 1- 3*. I blocked out the names for privacy reasons, but note the details.

2. <u>Didn't talk to the creditors on my terms:</u> If there is a time that the credit card company calls and you are not ready to talk, tell them they called you at a bad time and that you will call them back. This gives you time to set up your recorder and to look over your notes from the past conversations you had with them. From your notes, you will know information you have given them. Don't give them too much information; they may use it against you.

⚬━ KEY: Don't give information by saying, "Let me talk with a family member to see if they will loan me some money," or, "I plan on selling my car. Maybe I'll have some money after that." Keep all the communication as general as possible.

A big mistake I made was not talking on my terms. There was a time that I sold some items, had the money available to negotiate, and the credit card company called and caught me off guard.

I should have said, "You called me at a bad time," and asked for their extension number to call them back in a few minutes. Instead I took the call, and knowing I had money from selling items, negotiated over the phone without looking at my past notes. I went from memory which was a costly mistake because I had the wrong numbers for the wrong credit card company. If I had looked and taken the extra time to see what we'd talked about before, I could have saved hundreds of dollars. Therefore, always talk to the credit card companies when you are ready. Don't let them catch you off guard. Talk on your terms.

It is extremely important that you take detailed notes. Meticulous notes were very helpful and saved me thousands of dollars. See my conversation notes in *Appendix Pages 1-3*.

There was a time that one of the credit card companies (Capitol One) said that they would negotiate with me on a final payment. We agreed over the phone on a price. I repeated what the maximum amount would be for the payoff, how many months, and the amount of the payments. The representative agreed to it and said that he would fax me a copy of the agreement. He faxed it and when I looked at it, it was different than the others that I had seen. Since this was a different company I just thought maybe their form is a little different. That wasn't the case. The form he sent me was not what we had agreed to over the phone. We talked about a maximum amount to be paid off, but the representative had left that amount open on the form.

⚬━ KEY: Beware of false settlements. His plan was to come back after so many months and say that what I paid was only part of the agreement. See *Appendix Page 4* for a false settlement. BEWARE! Don't accept anything like this. Notice the line that says "and additional checks agreed to but not listed here due to space." There was no ceiling mentioned; it was left open on purpose.

See *Appendix Pages 5–8* for what a true settlement agreement should look like. Notice actual amounts are mentioned as settlement in full.

After I made all my payments, I contacted Capitol One for them to sign off, showing that the agreed settlement was paid in full. They would not; they said it was only a partial payment. I no longer sent them any payments, but I did have to hire a lawyer.

I had a phone conversation with the credit card representative who was trying to collect more money. He was asking about more payments and when I was going to send in more. I said that I'd paid everything that we'd agreed to. He said I still owed thousands of dollars. (*This is where the detailed notes came in.*) I told him exactly what dates we'd spoken, what the agreement was, and that they have a recording of it that I would like for them to play over the phone so we can both hear it again. The recording was in the archives (almost two years later), so it took them a while to find it. It was days before they called me back with the recording. When they did call back, it was interesting, the credit card company didn't play the whole conversation I had with the representative. They left out the important parts of the agreement. I told them over the phone that this was not the whole recording and then I read from my notes what had been agreed to. I didn't pay them any more money, but it was very helpful to go to the lawyer and get new information on my rights and what the law says about agreements.

See *Appendix Page 13*. This was a letter from my lawyer explaining Indiana legal theory called "accord and satisfaction." With this information I decided to wait and see what the credit card company would do. They ended up selling the note to a third party, which eventually sold it to a fourth party, which sold to a fifth party.

I didn't know that they (Capitol One) sold this note until I received something in the mail from the third party. This was many months later so I had forgotten about it, thinking that everything was ok.

Once I received the correspondence from the third party, I went back to my lawyer and had my lawyer send a letter explaining the law, the agreement that was made, and that I'd fulfilled my end of the agreement.

See *Appendix Page 9—10* for copies of the correspondence between lawyers.

After my lawyer sent the letter, I didn't hear from that credit card company or from the third party that bought it.

☛ **KEY:** Once again, the thing that helped me the most were the detailed notes that I took on every phone call and the recordings of those phone calls.

3. <u>Didn't leave money in savings long enough:</u> Another mistake that I made was taking money out of my savings, retirement account, and the children's college fund to make the normal, monthly payments. In the long run it didn't do me any good. It only prolonged the inevitable and delayed the problem a couple more months. I would have been better off to save that money and use it as part of the payoff settlement. By using it ahead of time, I didn't have anything to show for it. Using that money for the normal credit card payment took away from what I could pay on other bills.

☛ **KEY:** It is better not to touch your savings when you know you will be negotiating soon. Leave it alone, don't mention it to the credit card companies, and use it as a last resort when it comes time to make the settlement payments.

As a side note, I was scared that my children wouldn't be able to go to college because I'd used their college fund. It wasn't a whole lot, but it could have gotten them a couple of semesters of school. It was interesting, my first child went to college and because our income was so low, she was able to get grants and loans in her name. At the end of the first year she sat out a year and worked a job. She was able to pay her loans off within that year. She then went to another college and again was able to get grants and loans. She is now working to pay off the loans, which should be paid off in the next 12 months.

My son, who also had a small college fund, was able to go to a university on scholarships, grants, and loans. Again, with our income being low, he was able to get the government grants. It surprised me that the scholarships that he received were far more than any amount that I had set aside for him. I was very thankful for the scholarships. I guess I didn't need to be scared in the first place.

4. Didn't stagger payments: You should staggered a few of the last payments instead of not paying all the creditors all at once. Allow me to explain.

When I drew a "line in the sand," deciding not to live off of credit cards, I stopped my credit card payments all at once. I had been current for the previous thirty years, but without enough cash coming in I couldn't pay the necessary bills and the credit cards also. As I look back, if I had made a minimum payment on a couple of them, that would have kept me current for another month. Then the following month, I could have made a minimum payment on only one of the cards. That would have made me current a month longer with that card company. That would have delayed some of the phone calls from the creditors. Plus, that would have given me more time to come up with more money. As long as the account is current, the creditors won't call. It's only when they don't receive payment that they start calling. The above payment plan would have staggered or delayed the contact from a few of the creditors instead of having all of them calling at once.

5. Didn't sell excess items soon enough: I took too long in selling excess items. This is mentioned in much more detail in the *Sell, Sell, Sell* chapter, but it is worth mentioning here.

The key is to prepare for the future. In a few months you will need to make some payment arrangements with the credit card company. You need to GET READY! Once you stop making payments, the clock is ticking. It is important that you no longer worry about interest rates, late fees, credit scores, etc. Start piling up as much cash as possible so that you will have something to negotiate with. The credit card companies want cash and they would rather settle with some cash instead of writing it off with no cash. Again, they want cash instead of selling the loan for pennies on the dollar to a third party. So get ready!

☛ **KEY:** Don't pay on the credit cards until the credit card companies are ready to settle. This statement is worth repeating—**don't pay on the credit cards until the credit card companies are ready to settle!** Make sure you have a valid settlement agreement before you send any payments. Also, you will need to keep good records of what has been sent to the credit card company.

(Copies of valid settlement agreements can be seen at *Appendix Pages 5–8, 18, 25.*)

6. Didn't communicate when needed: This one cost me a lot of worry and loss of sleep. I thought I lost hundreds of dollars in payments made. I was making my payments as agreed, to a particular credit card company. They wanted me to contact them every six months, coinciding with the automatic withdrawal agreement the credit card company had arranged. At the end of the six months they would usually call me and ask if I would increase the payment. They would ask for an additional $50—$100.

BEWARE: Credit card companies will do this. They will ask for an increase of payment so the note gets paid off sooner. Only agree to what you can do. Don't commit to something you can't keep. If you can't increase the amount, then keep it the same. Most of the time, I was not able to increase the payments because of all the bills I had. A couple of times I was able to increase it by $5 or $10 and the credit card companies were ok with that. Then they set up the payments for another six months.

Here is the big mistake I made: after six months I didn't call the creditors. I didn't think too much of it; I got busy with other things and usually they called me. Well, I was putting money in the account for them to pull it out automatically, but the first month I didn't notice they hadn't pulled it out. The second month, I put money into the account for the payment and by the end of the month the money was still there. I finally called and told them that the money was in the account but they didn't withdraw it. Here's where it got scary. The creditor told me that they no longer had the account, but they had passed it on to a third party. They said that they had tried to call me about it, but they hadn't. My guess is that some representative just marked on his/her paper that they tried to call but never did.

I was very concerned because of all the payments that I had made (over $9,000) and I was close to paying off the final agreement. My concern was not knowing if the new third party would recognize all the money that I'd paid. I kept telling the new creditor that the money had always been in the account and that the credit card company didn't withdraw it. The money had been there!

After going through my statements and listing all the payments that I had paid and deposits made, the new third party company agreed to withdraw the money to bring the account current. They allowed me to continue to make monthly payments as I did before without showing any missed payments. This was huge since I had already paid thousands of dollars! I didn't want to start over. I was afraid that I had lost over $9,000 in payments.

☞ KEY: I did find out that some of these companies have subsidiaries that pass the account around. A person may think they are dealing with one company for a while, then later get correspondence in the mail from a different company. Be sure to double check the addresses and see if they are coming from the same place under different names. (See a sample of that at *Appendix Page 11*. Pay attention to all the different business names that they use.)

Back to the mistake. I should have called the creditor as soon as I realized that the money wasn't withdrawn like it should have been. This would have saved me a lot of stress, loss of sleep, loss of time, and extra work pulling together all the payments that I had made.

7. <u>Told my lawyer I had a large down payment available:</u> I let my lawyer do the negotiating. It got to a point that I wasn't able to work with one of the credit card companies.

They got their lawyers involved which caused me to hire my lawyer. The mistake I made was letting my lawyer know that I could make a nice size down payment then make a nice size final payment. I should have kept the arrangements to lower monthly payments and not mention what I could do. Once the credit card company discovered what I could afford, they would not back down. Therefore, through my lawyer, I couldn't negotiate any payments because I'd suggested a strong commitment earlier. I should have told them a smaller down payment and worked out a payment plan over the next six months, instead I made two large payments. I was thankful that I sold some items and had the money to make the payments.

8. Didn't pay the IRS first: There are a few things that I learned that will be helpful to share with others. As I look back, I realize I made a mistake by not paying the IRS first. I should have made that my first priority. I may have been thinking I had more time before the IRS would contact me, or thinking because it deals with my business account I'll wait until later. Maybe I was so overwhelmed that I let it go. Either way I should have taken care of my back taxes before paying on the credit cards.

8a) The IRS will not call you.

They always send correspondence by mail.

BEWARE: There are scam artist that claim they are with the IRS trying to help you clear up a tax problem and they want to gather your valuable information over the phone. That may include personal identification information such as social security number and credit card info for some type of payment. The IRS will not call.

Please note, there was a time that the State of Indiana called me (concerning a business account) and left a message on my voice mail. At first, I ignored the message. It was about the third call from them before I took them seriously enough to return the call.

When I did get a hold of them, I let them tell me the information they had on file instead of me giving them any information, because I wanted to verify that the call was for real.

8b) The IRS was easy to deal with on a short-term payment plan.

When I spoke with the representative of the IRS, he was very nice. This was totally different from the credit card creditors. He took my information, I explained what had happened and he asked me if I could pay the amount due over the next three months. He asked, if it would work in my budget. As I crunched the numbers I said it would. He told me that I would receive something in the mail in the next two weeks. He also said that payments can be made daily, weekly or monthly toward the balance. A voucher was sent with all the important information, including tax numbers. This voucher was important to send with the payment so the funds would be credited to the right account. I made the payments over the next three months which took care of the back taxes.

I have seen on the state level, that if, (with a business,) you miss sending in with-holding tax, sales tax, or the year end WH-1 tax form, that the state will send you a notice. It may take 6-10 months before you get the notice, but they will track you down. The notice may have an inflated price on it. That number may be hundreds of dollars more than what you truly owe. I guess they are trying to get your attention and shock you into action.

From my experience, just fill out the right paperwork and submit the forms to the right place with any payment that may be due. If that doesn't satisfy them, they may want more paperwork or you may need to hire an accountant to help clear things up. Usually an accountant is less expensive than a lawyer.

8c) The IRS will charge penalties and interest.

The interest may go back to day one, compounded daily, from when the forms were due. The penalty is a flat rate, usually 10%. If a person has to set a payment plan, there may be a one-time set up fee. This fee could be from $40 -$110. If a person fails to make the payments on time, there may also be a fee to reinstate the agreement. After a while those fees will add up.

You may be able to negotiate some or all of the fees.

I remember one time I forgot to file an annual report on the Federal level. Eventually I received a notice in the mail that I owed money with penalties and interest. I called the IRS explained what had happened, that I totally forgot to file the form. For this form, if I would have filed on time, the balance would have been zero taxes due. After talking with the representative, he was able to waive all the fees if I would submit the paperwork. So I did.

The story doesn't end there. A couple of years later I forgot to file that same annual report. Once again I received a notice that I owed money along with penalties and interest. If I would have filed on time, there were no taxes due, but because I didn't file, there were fees. I called the IRS representative and asked if they could help me out by removing the penalty and interest. The representative looked at my history and found that somebody had waived the fees a couple of years earlier. Because of that they would not do it again. It was a tough lesson to learn...file the paperwork on time!

8d) Filing bankruptcy doesn't eliminate your tax bill.

As I considered bankruptcy, my lawyer said that just because a person files bankruptcy, it does not remove the tax bill. The IRS wants their money. They may negotiate on the amount, but they still want their money.

If they sense a person is avoiding them and is not willing to pay their tax bill or make arrangements to pay back taxes, the IRS may start the collection process. You don't want it to go that far. They can levy a person's assets. In turn, the IRS may put the assets up for auction and get what money they can out of the assets. If it doesn't bring enough money the IRS may still charge the taxpayer for the remaining balance. Remember interest is being charged on a daily basis.

It would be better if the person needing to pay the tax bill, sells the item or items themselves and give the money to the IRS. This concept of selling items is mentioned in chapter 6; *Sell, Sell, Sell*.

8e) IRS.GOV

When dealing with the IRS you can go to **IRS.GOV.** This web site is very helpful. There is a section on **Know Your Rights**. Under that is a sub-section **Taxpayer Bill of Rights.** All these sections have helpful information. If you wonder about collections, there is also a section on **Collection Process for Taxpayers Filing and or Paying Late.** Again, that is at **IRS.GOV.**

I hope you have found this chapter helpful. I don't want you to make the same mistakes I did. Some of those mistakes cost me hundreds, if not thousands, of dollars. That's one reason I wrote this book, to help prevent that from happening to others. As I was going through this process of negotiating with the credit card companies, I didn't have a guide like this book to tell me what to do and what not to do. Everything was uncharted territory for me and I didn't know what to expect. As I look back, there were plenty of mistakes I made. I hope you, as the reader, take note of them so the same mistakes are not repeated, which in turn can cost somebody hundreds of dollars, if not thousands, like it did me.

Now let's move to a happier subject: *Things I Did Right.*

☛ Key Summary:
- **Don't give extra information in your responses. Keep all communication as general as possible.**
- **Beware of false settlements.**
- **Take detailed notes and record phone calls.**
- **Do not touch your savings when negotiating.**
- **Do not pay the credit cards until the credit card companies are ready to settle.**
- **Pay attention to all the different business names a company uses.**
- **Pay the IRS first!**

---

3. Things I Did Right

Thankfully it wasn't all mistakes going through my process. There were many things I did that benefited me and saved thousands of dollars.

A few of the things that I did right:

1. Kept control myself and didn't consolidate
2. Opened a different checking account
3. Kept the same phone number
4. Had open communication with card companies
5. Followed through on the commitments
6. Took very detailed notes
7. Had a phone recorder
8. Sold items
9. Hired a lawyer

I may be repeating some of this information, but it is worth repeating. Doing the right thing can save you hundreds of dollars.

1. Kept control myself and didn't consolidate: I kept control of my accounts, even though there were quite a number of credit card companies to manage. I did consider hiring a consolidation firm. A consolidation firm is somebody that says they deal with the creditors on my behalf. I'm sure there may be some honest ones out there, but I didn't know who to trust. I didn't want to be sending my money to somebody I didn't know in hopes that they would pay my bill for me. Their claim was that they may get a reduction of 30–50% of what was owed. I was able to save 50—80% in some cases myself. I felt that I would have a better concern for my own account than somebody else would, so I just kept control and didn't go through a consolidation company.

2. Opened a different checking account: I opened a separate checking account. I didn't want to mix my personal everyday transactions with the creditors. I also didn't want them to have access to more money than they were allowed, so I opened a separate checking account at a separate bank / credit union, totally different from the main checking account. I didn't want the confusion of having two different checking accounts at the same bank. I kept only a minimum amount of money in there, just enough money for the payments to clear. It is important that you keep an eye on this. I did have a time where the creditor took out double payments in one month. This caused a lot of problems because I didn't have enough money in the account for the second transaction. That caused overdraft fees and additional charges. I called the creditor and told them what they did. They were very fast in getting it corrected and they paid for the extra fees. There may have been another recourse that I could have taken, but I didn't pursue anything. I was glad that they paid the overdraft fees. The key is to watch your balance carefully so you know how much is going in, how much is being taken out, and who is taking the funds out.

3. <u>Kept the same phone number:</u> I kept the same phone number, although it was a pain—a major pain. I was getting phone calls all the time, even on Sundays. I would look at caller ID and know the creditor on the other end. I wanted them to be able to call me and to know I was still around.

   ☛ **KEY:** When somebody changes their phone number the creditor may assume that they left town, moved away and that they don't want to work with them. This way, I tried to keep open communication. I didn't answer the phone every time, but it would at least go into voicemail. That way they could leave a message if they wanted to.

4. <u>Had open communication with card companies:</u> Open communication is very important. The next whole chapter is on this subject. If the credit card company senses that you don't want to work with them, they may sell the balance you owe them to a third party. It is far better to work with the original card company than a third party who doesn't care about your past payment history.

5. <u>Followed through on the commitments:</u> Follow through is extremely important. I will go into more detail in the communication chapter. When I came to terms with the credit card company, I would follow through with the agreements. If I said I was going to make a payment by a certain date, I would do it. If I said that I was going to mail a payment by a certain date, I would do it. There were times I would call the creditor and tell them that I put a payment in the mail on a certain date, with the check number and the amount of the check. If I made a deposit into my checking account or at one of their branches, I would call them and let them know the money was in the account.

   ☛ **KEY:** Along with open communication is follow through. Please note that when I say open communication, I am not saying tell the credit card companies everything. Most details you need to keep very general. What I mean by open communication is keeping the phone number current, and every so often, talk to a representative and try to negotiate a settlement.

6. <u>Took very detailed notes:</u> I would take extensive notes after every conversation. There was a time that my lawyer wrote a letter to a law firm explaining the meticulous notes that I took. What the lawyer said was that if we had to go to court, my notes were so detailed that I would have the advantage over their notes. I found that many times the credit card company representatives took very poor notes. If I called and asked for a certain person that I dealt with in the past, and that person was out for the day, the new representative would have trouble reading over the notes and wouldn't be able to understand what had been discussed. One time it was so bad that the creditor didn't know if they had called the right number or if I was the right person that they needed to talk with. That case took a number of weeks to figure out, but we finally figured out what they were referencing and eventually came to terms. I say all that so you know the importance of taking good notes. It takes time, but it can save you time and money in the long run. After the phone call I would go to the computer and record the date, the time of day, and how long we talked, and sometimes how long they left me on hold. I would also write down the name of the person or people I spoke to and I would get their extension number in case we got disconnected. Sometimes the first representative would pass me on to somebody else. I would keep track of the supervisor's name so I would know who to ask for next time. The supervisor would be able to negotiate a deeper discount than what the first representative would be able to. Knowing this, you can by-pass the others and go to the supervisor directly. I found that even the supervisor would need to go to a manager. So the higher up in the chain you get, the better off you are. Each time I would talk with somebody, I would write it down. Even if the person I was calling wasn't there, I would record who I talked with and what was said. This is a very valuable principle.

7. <u>Had a phone recorder:</u> At the beginning of the phone conversation, the calling party will say that this phone call is being recorded and that they are gathering information trying to collect a debt. You can agree to that and at the same time you can say, "I am recording this conversation on my end as well."

I didn't have a phone conversation recorder at first. Eventually, I did get one and it was very helpful. I was able to use it to replay the conversation, so I could play back the details as I put them into the computer.

☛ **KEY:** There are different types of phone recorders; any one will work. The one I used had micro cassette tapes. I would write on them which company I was talking with and what dates. I would have a different tape for each company. There are also digital recorders that will work over the phone. You will need to do some research and see what is on the market and what is in your price range. I bought one from Radio Shack and the original list price was $99.00. I was able to buy it on sale for under $20.00 and it worked very well. Do your research, but **don't** start this process without one. This is a very valuable tool! A must have!

8. <u>Sold items:</u> I sold items on E-bay or social media. This allows you to start stockpiling cash. To do this, you need to take inventory of everything you can sell—anything that has value, and the sooner you sell it (within the first 3 months of missed payments), the better off you will be. Look around at your inventory. Make a list on paper. Go from room to room, upstairs, downstairs, in the attic, in the shed, in the storage unit, in the garage, and wherever else you may have items and put them on the list. Your list may consist of extra tools, extra cars, coins, stamp collections, toys, motorbikes, boats, snowmobiles, trailers, campers, garage sale items, and anything that may sell on E-bay, Craigslist, garage sales, flea markets, etc. Although I sold items on E-bay, I should have started sooner. See more information concerning this topic under the *Sell, Sell, Sell* chapter.

9. <u>Hired a lawyer:</u> I hired a lawyer when the need arose. I went to a bankruptcy lawyer. Although he suggested that my wife and I file bankruptcy, we didn't feel that was the thing to do. We wanted to work with the creditors as much as possible. Filing bankruptcy was one area I didn't want to go. It may have been easier on my wife and myself, because of all the stress, the phone calls, the liquidating of assets, but we decided not to file bankruptcy.

The lawyer was very helpful in explaining what to do or not do in certain scenarios. Such as when to answer the creditor and when not to. I remember a time we went to his office and I explained about the most current card company and where we were in the negotiation process. I then mentioned there were five or six more right behind it but they weren't as far along in the process as the others. He said we will take them one at a time if need be. Otherwise, he told me, that I may be able to negotiate with them myself. He was right, with most of them I was able to negotiate myself. Therefore, I didn't need to have him write letters or contact them on my behalf.

One of the credit card companies, Discover, was very quick in filing a lawsuit against me. I tried to work with them ahead of time, but I didn't have the money to settle with them. I hoped that Discover would sell the balance to a third party, which would have allowed me some more time to pull together some money, but they didn't. They hired a lawyer and filed a case in the local court system.

I learned about it when a local deputy came to my house and delivered papers to my door, the last known address that the credit card company had on file, which was still my current address. The sheriff delivered the papers letting me know that there was a court hearing and I was being sued.

I knew the sheriff that delivered the court papers to my house. I saw him at a repair shop one day so I stopped to ask him about the paperwork. He told me that "Discover was the hardest card company to negotiate with and that they file in court very quickly. It's not easy to work with them after so many months. They take people to court as quickly as possible." The sheriff later told me all month long his days were spent delivering court papers. He also told me I may want to hire a lawyer in this situation. So I did.

My Discover card had about a $12,000 balance. My wife and I decided to work with Discover as much as we could. With the help of my lawyer, we were able to delay the proceedings for a while. It came down to the final days and I was expecting that I would need $8,000 to settle or have to let it drag out in court. I didn't have the $8,000 or anything near that so that wasn't an option. Although I tried to borrow the money, all the doors were shut. I asked my lawyer if he could negotiate with the lawyers that Discover had hired. Those lawyers knew that my lawyer was a bankruptcy lawyer so they knew that bankruptcy could be a possibility. My lawyer called them and worked out a plan. My lawyer reported to me that I didn't need any down payment and the lawyers for Discover would take $200 per month payment for the next nine months then the payments would increase to $400 per month until it was paid off. There would also be an 8% interest on the note. I felt 8% was a lot better than the 23–27% the card company was charging me.

The good thing was that I didn't have to come up with any down payment. Sometimes the firms or credit card companies want a nice down payment to show a strong commitment to a repayment plan. I was relieved that I could go with monthly payments. The lawyer told me if I could get some money saved up and then offer them a reduced settlement, they might take it. I ended up paying the full $12,000 plus 8% interest, plus court fees. This was the only case that I had to pay the full amount plus interest and court cost. With all of the other card companies, I was able to negotiate for sometimes pennies on the dollar. As I look back, I should have tried to settle quicker with Discover before it went to the lawyers' hands. I may have been able to keep it out of the court system and settle for a lower amount. I didn't realize how fast Discover takes their cases to the courts.

Once all the payments were completed and the agreement was settled, I received a "Satisfaction & Release of Judgment" letter. For a copy of that letter, see *Appendix Page 12*. Again, I marked out the actual case number and the lawyers name, but the letter will give you an idea what to look for if the case is taken to court.

The "Satisfaction & Release of Judgment" letter is something to keep on file for the rest of your life! I found out that Discover never contacted the credit bureau to explain that the case has been paid in full. So, more than two years later, I am stilling dealing with that, submitting paperwork and trying to get what appears to be an open judgment off my credit report.

I felt that I needed to hire a lawyer to work out a payment plan on my behalf since Discover submitted it to their lawyers and were starting the process of taking me to court.

There are times when you may need to hire a lawyer. Hiring your own lawyer may get better results than trying to do it by yourself, especially when it ends up in court.

There were two other times when I had to hire a lawyer. One time was when the credit card company, Capitol One, lied to me and tried to get more money than what our agreement was.

After I made all my payments, I contacted Capitol One for them to sign it off, showing that the agreed settlement was paid in full. They would not; they said it was only a partial payment. I no longer sent them any payments.

The account was settled according to the agreement, but later I received a letter in the mail from an unknown lawyer asking for more money.

I found it interesting that a number of months after I finished my correspondence with Capitol One and their lawyers, this letter came. See *Appendix Page 14*.

The letter was from another creditor regarding the same account about 8 months later. I'm guessing that the lawyer sold the account to a fourth party creditor. The lawyer knew the account was satisfied so he sold it to somebody else. I sent the fourth-party collector a letter, explaining the agreement and how I wished that Capitol One would have been honest with them. See *Appendix Page 15*. It took a couple of letters back and forth but I didn't hear from that lawyer again. At the time of this writing, the third- or fourth-party creditor has not proceeded with any other communication.

☞ **KEY:** Beware of Capitol One! From my experience, I have found them to be liars, deceptive, and very hard to work with. Since then, I have received a letter requesting more money, which is probably from a fifth party collection agency. I found the letters interesting how they themselves recognize that the original loan was past the statue of limitations. See *Appendix Page 32*.

It is very interesting that Capital One and Discover keep offering me a credit card in the mail. I must be on their new list that says I have good credit and they want me to be a credit card customer. That is very interesting to me.

I hope you don't make the same mistakes I have. I wrote this chapter to help guide you on some things I did right, which could save you a lot of time, stress, and money.

☞ Key Summary:
- **Keep open communication.**
- **Follow through on commitments.**
- **Any phone recorder will work, just get one.**
- **Beware of Capitol One.**

---

4. Communication / Negotiation / Follow Through

Communication

This is a very important topic when dealing with the creditors. **Communication, negotiation,** and **follow through** are critical. Each item is very important and worth taking the time to discuss in detail.

Once my wife and I "drew a line in the sand" and said we are not going to live off credit cards, I had to decide if I was going to keep control of the accounts or try and hire somebody to manage them for me. I looked at different possibilities of debt consolidation companies but the stories I heard were not positive. They were middlemen wanting paid for their services. I don't see a problem with that, but I was concerned if they would care about my accounts as much as I did. I felt that I would care about my accounts better than they would. I didn't want to send money to a third party not knowing if they would send it to the right creditor. I also didn't know if they could get the best deal for me. They said 30–50% savings, but I found out that some of the credit card companies gave me up to an 80% savings.

☞ **KEY:** I decided to keep control of all my accounts. That meant dealing with each creditor when they called (sometimes they were very rude), doing the faxing, mailing in payments or making deposits through the bank or Western Union, and calling the creditor to communicate when checks were sent or when deposits were made.

As I kept control, one thing I did was to keep the same phone number. Many times I thought about having the phone number changed, but keeping the same number was a way the creditors could get in touch with me. This way they knew that I didn't move locations or think that I was trying to avoid them.

After the first couple of months of missed payments the phone calls started coming, sometimes daily. There were times we would even get calls on Sundays. I wanted to work with each credit card company, but didn't have the money. Because of the recession I had lost approximately 70% of my income. I couldn't keep paying the card companies and keep food on the table and a roof over my head.

I asked the card companies to lower the interest rate, but they wouldn't. I tried to explain that I didn't have the money.

After missing four or five payments, I started to receive letters from the card companies along with the phone calls. I started to send letters back. I explained my situation and I also sent a family picture showing the members of our family. I admitted that I owe some money and asked in a kind way if they could show grace and mercy by forgiving the debt that I owed. I offered to start making payments once I got back on my feet, but I didn't have any idea when that would be. I apologized for not being able to pay, but I wanted to work with them. See *Appendix Page 16* for a copy of the letter that I wrote.

Negotiation

After about six months of missed payments, phone calls, and correspondence, I was able to start negotiating with the card companies. I wish I had started to sell items of value before this time so I could have dealt with more of the creditors in a timely matter, but I didn't. I negotiated with as many as I could. Usually they didn't want to talk with me until the account was five to seven months past due.

Part of the negotiating would be coming to an agreement that both parties could accept. They tried to get as much money as possible but I didn't have any to pay them so we would need to come to an agreement.

If their offer was reasonable, both with the amount of money and with the time frame, which would allow me to pull money together, I would accept their offer.

Here were some offers that I accepted after we negotiated. The credit card companies sent me letters and I responded by sending the credit card companies letters. It seemed to be in the five to nine-month range after not paying anything that I was able to get these offers. Once again, I was dealing with the original companies before they would have sold the balance to a third party.

I must add this disclaimer: I am only able to share with you my experience of negotiating with the creditors, I cannot guarantee or suggest that you will get the same results.

Card Company A	Debt of $18,187.44	settled for $3,700
Card Company B	Debt of $16,608.79	settled for $2,000
Card Company C	Debt of $18,129.46	settled for $2,000
Card Company D	Debt of $27,077.37	settled for $8,123.22
Card Company E	Debt of $10,362.00	settled for $3,040
Card Company F	Debt of $19,343.59	settled for $10,000
Card Company G	Debt of $8,789.90	settled for $4,598
Card Company H	Debt of $20,967.00	settled for $13,000
Card Company I	Debt of $1,077.57	settled for $550

I had ten major credit cards, all with large balances. Above are nine companies I was able to negotiate with, regarding the amount I would pay back and the time frame in which I could do that.

☛ **KEY:** I can't say this enough. At the sixth-, seventh-, or eight-month time frame, the credit card company is getting ready to sell the unpaid balance to a third party. Sometimes they are sold to lawyers, investment companies or other banking firms. The third party may feel that they can buy the balance for pennies on the dollar, hoping to take somebody to court for the full amount. With this in mind, it's highly recommended that you work with the main credit card company. They have had your account the longest and you have paid them the most interest, therefore they are more willing to cut a deal with you than if a third party buys the unpaid loan. The deal the credit card company cuts, may be pennies on the dollar or may even be more than what they would sell it to a third party. I was able to get the above-mentioned payoffs, with the people that I dealt with in the first nine months. These are actual agreements that I worked out with the credit card companies.

It is also important to know what a true agreement letter looks like. See *Appendix Pages 5-8* for some true agreement letters that will hold up in court if it ever had to go that far. The names have been marked out but the words of the letter are what to look for.

Appendix Page 4 is a fake agreement, a false settlement that the credit card company sent me. I was not aware at the time that this was a fake agreement. It left the payment plan open and didn't report on the letter the maximum amount of money it would take to settle the account as agreed on the phone. It was a good thing that I took detailed notes and that I had a phone recorder to back up the verbal agreement that was made. This was one for which I had to hire a lawyer, more than once, to get them off my back. This took over two years before the third-party creditor dropped the account.

Notice that they put an open ended statement: "additional checks agreed to but not listed here due to space." That is so they can come back and say I owe more money. My thought is, if they needed more space, they could have put it on two pages.

That's why it is important to know what is a true settlement letter and what is not. Knowing ahead of time can save you thousands of dollars and a lot of time and lawyer fees.

As I look back, I realize I should not have accepted the agreement letter because it didn't have the full agreement spelled out per the phone conversation between the credit card representative and myself. I should have made them rewrite it according to the agreement we made over the phone, then re-fax it to me before I started paying on it. I thought it wouldn't be a problem since everything was recorded, but I was wrong. In fact, when I asked the company to replay the recording, it took a couple of days for them to find it in the archives. When they did play the recording for me, they left out the part where the representative was explaining how the agreement would work and that all payments would go toward the balance of the agreement amount. How convenient for them to cut out the most important part.

With the other credit card companies, there were times that I didn't agree with the settlement amount either because I felt that they could do better or because I didn't have the money to make a commitment to them. Because of this, the credit card company would keep calling. Remember that there is a time frame that the credit card companies are dealing with. They can't keep an open balance on their books too long. So if we didn't come to an agreement, the clock was still ticking.

☛ **KEY:** It is always better to deal with the original credit card company instead of the third party company that they may sell your account to.

After negotiating back and forth, we would come to an agreement. The other thing that helped was that I was able to stall for time, which allowed me to sell more items to get more money. The money then allowed me to make a firm commitment to the creditor.

☛ **KEY:** I found that the representatives liked to have an agreement in place by Saturday, if not Friday. Many times it seemed they would have a meeting with their supervisor on Mondays explaining what they were able to do the week before. That was on a weekly basis.

I also found that on a monthly basis the credit card company wanted the agreement to be in place by the 24th of the month. They may give a person until the end of the month to pay and stretch the payments out over a number of months, but they wanted a strong commitment by the 24th. I think they needed to decide by the end of the month if they were going to keep the account on their books or sell it. If no progress is being made, they may talk about court actions.

The credit card company may consider what month it is when they are going to negotiate with you. Let me explain.

I had a case in which we were able to negotiate in July of that year. I assumed that they would want it off their books by the end of the year, so I asked them for a five month payment plan, which they agreed to. That way it was off their books before January.

One thing concerning the end of year is that the January following the year in which you make the final payment, you may get a 1099-C. This is a form showing that the credit card company wrote off a certain amount of money and you have to report it on your taxes. Therefore, you may owe some income tax on the amount that was written off.

☞ **KEY:** Whenever $600.00 or more of debt is forgiven as a result of settling a debt for less than the balance owing, the creditor is required to report the amount of the debt forgiven to the Internal Revenue Service on a 1099-C form, a copy of which would be mailed to you by the creditor. If you are uncertain of the legal or tax consequences, I encourage you to consult your legal or tax advisor.

See *Appendix Pages 28-31* for some samples of the 1099-C Forms that I received. Looking back at the past years, I realized that in one year I received over $35,400 in 1099-C. Another year I received over $28,000 in 1099-C. Each time I had to report them on my taxes as income and pay additional money for the taxes that were due.

One thing to consider with the payoff dates and the year in which the amount is paid off, is how it will affect your tax filing status. Ask yourself, "what happens if I receive several 1099-C Forms in the same year?" It could affect the amount you owe to the IRS the next tax season. This could create another problem, so be aware of what year you make your final payment and what tax year the 1099-C may arrive.

The example above, having the settlement paid off in December, was better for me than to wait and have it paid off in January. There was a case where it was better for me to go the extra month into the next year for the final payment. The reason would be because I knew that there would be a large amount on the 1099-C and I would not be able to pay the taxes due that upcoming year. Therefore, I delayed the taxes due by 12-15 months, all because I finished the last payment in January or February instead of December. I say all that just so you are aware what a difference a month can make, especially when there may be taxes due.

Once I was able to come to terms, I would set up a payment plan. There were some companies I was able to pay all at once with one payment. With others, I had to make two or three payments. Others, I had to work out a payment plan of twenty-four to forty-eight months. One of them took me to court and the lawyers worked out the interest and a payment plan. Most of the time the credit card companies didn't charge any interest, they just wanted payments and to get it off their books.

I noticed that the credit card companies tried to get as large of a down payment as possible. Sometimes I couldn't manage that. Therefore, I would negotiate two equal payments. Other times it would be three equal payments. If I had some cash on hand, I would make a down payment. This would show I was serious about the commitment I was making, then after that I would make the monthly payments until the end of the agreement.

Making the payments took on different forms. Depending on the arrangements, sometimes I would go to the Western Union office and transmit the money that way. See *Appendix Page 17* for a copy of the Western Union form. Sometimes I would take it to one of the branches of the bank I was dealing with. The credit card company would have me put the money in a special account with a reference number then I would need to call the credit card company and tell them the day I made the deposit. That way, the credit card company would check the deposits that day and match the amount I gave them and credit it to my account. Other times I would write a check and send it by mail, sometimes certified. I had to have the check to their office by a certain day or I would be penalized. If the mail delivery date would be close, I would call the creditor to let them know I put a check in the mail on such and such a date, for what amount, and what the check number was. The other way was to allow the credit card company to withdraw funds from my checking account.

I went to a different bank/credit union and opened a second checking account that was totally different from my personal everyday account. I didn't want the confusion of having two different checking accounts at the same bank.

I knew that if I gave the credit card companies my account number and routing number, they would have access to my account and may pull out more money than what was authorized. This did happen once, but it was cleared up quickly. I found out about it because I would only keep a minimum amount of money in the checking account, just enough money for the payments to clear. It is important that you keep an eye on this. When the creditor took out a double payment in one month, this caused a lot of problems because I didn't have enough money in the account for the second transaction. It caused overdraft fees and additional charges. I called the creditor and told them what they did. They were very fast in getting it corrected and they paid for the extra fees. There may have been more recourse that I could have taken, but I didn't pursue anything. I was glad that they paid the overdraft fees.

☛ **KEY:** The key is to be sure to watch your balance carefully, so you know how much is going in, how much is taken out, and who is taking the funds out.

This is worth repeating: Don't give the credit card companies access to your main checking account. Keep it separate.

Follow Through

This is very important. If you have already negotiated and come to an agreement then there has been a lot of phone calls, rude conversations from the credit card representatives, loss of sleep, and a lot stress.

This is where the follow through is important. Whatever arrangements have been made, I hope you have good notes in your file. Now, mark out the calendar when the payments are due and where they are going to be sent or delivered. Keep track if the creditor is pulling the money out of your account or if you need to make a deposit or send a check. Be sure that if you are mailing something that you give the post office plenty of time to deliver the payment. Sometimes I would send the payment out by certified mail so I knew the credit card company received it on time. Many times, once the payment was in the mail, I would call the creditor to let them know the payment was on its way. You don't want late payments. That could void the whole settlement agreement.

I mentioned this elsewhere in the book, but there was a time that the automatic payments were not being removed from the checking account; the money was there but there was miscommunication. I didn't call the credit card company after the six month period to have them reset the monthly payments for the next six months. When I caught the problem and called the creditor, it was too late and the balance was already passed on to another third party.

I had made thirty-six payments to the creditor. I paid off almost 75% of the agreement, and then missed two payments, but not because the money wasn't there. I had put the money in the account. The payments were missed because the creditor didn't withdraw the money. Their program wasn't reset to withdraw the money for the next six months. When they passed the balance on to another debt collection company, it created a lot of stress. I didn't know if I had lost all of the payments and had to start over or if they would take me to court. I didn't know what to expect.

I called the creditor that I was dealing with and they said they passed it on to another debt collector, which they then gave me the name. I called the new creditor and explained what had happened, how the money was in the account but the payments weren't reset. They looked at the account and saw all the payments that were made. What I found out was that I was now dealing with a subsidiary of the other company. This new debt collector recognized all the payments so I was able to continue where I left off. They took the two months' payment out of the account right away, then put me back on a payment plan. Because I was dealing with a different company, they charged me an extra $7 per month transaction fee. I was willing to pay that if they were willing to recognize all the payments that had been made. I was able to sleep better that night once everything was back on schedule.

It would have been a lot easier and a lot less stressful if I had called right away, as soon as I'd noticed the creditor hadn't taken out the money the first month.

I say all of this to make sure you follow through to the last payment. If you happen to miss one payment or if they don't pull the money out of your account, call the creditor right away.

Once you have made all of the payments, you need to get a letter of satisfaction. It may also be called a "Settlement Paid in Full" letter. If you went through the court system, it would be called "Satisfaction and Release of Judgment." This is very, very important. You need to keep this in your file for the rest of your life. This is showing that the creditor has been satisfied with the agreement. They are saying that you made all the payments according to the agreement.

See *Appendix Pages 5-8 and 18* for some actual copies of the settlement letters.

Once I made the final payments, I usually had to write and ask for the "Settlement Paid in Full" letter. Sometimes the creditor would fax it to me; sometimes they would mail it to me. Because I had hired a lawyer to represent me in the court case, once the judgment was paid in full, the Satisfaction and Release letter was sent to my lawyer.

☞ **KEY:** These documents are important to keep on hand. There was a time that one of the debt collectors said I owed more money, and that they were expecting payment. It was a credit card company that I had already settled with, made the payments to, and received a Settlement Paid in Full letter. Because I had that, I was able to write back to the debt collector and send them a copy of the letter and tell them that the balance was satisfied. Once they received the letter, I didn't hear anymore from them.

At the time of this writing, I recently checked my credit report, only to find out that the judgment is still showing an open status against me. I will need to send in copies of the Satisfaction and Release of Judgment statements to the credit bureaus to get that resolved. It doesn't look good on my report even though it has been satisfied.

Credit Bureaus

For your information there are three credit bureaus. They are:

Equifax Consumer Relations
PO Box 740241
Atlanta, GA 30374–0193
www.Equifax.com
1–800–685–1111

Experian Consumer Relations
PO Box 2002
Allen, TX 75013
www.Experian.com
1–888–397–3742

TransUnion Consumer Relations
PO Box 1000
Chester, PA 19022
www.TransUnion.com
1–800–888–4213

For Free Annual Credit Report
www.annualcreditreport.com
1-877-FACT-ACT

You can request a copy of your credit report free of charge once a year from each one of the credit bureaus. If you want to keep a close watch on your reports, request a report every four months from a different bureau. For example, request a report from Equifax in the first part of the year, request a report from Experian four months later, then request a report from TransUnion four months after that. That will get you through the year, and then start over. If there is any inaccurate or incomplete information on the report, you have the right to dispute the matter with the reporting agency.

KEY: It is important to keep your credit report accurate.

Key Summary:
- **Keep control of all your accounts.**
- **Negotiate with the main credit card company.**
- **Deal with the original credit card company instead of the third party company.**
- **Representatives like having an agreement in place by Friday or Saturday.**
- **The creditor is required to report the amount of the debt forgiven to the Internal Revenue Service on a 1099-C form.**
- **Watch your balance carefully**
- **Keep the Satisfaction and Release letters on hand, forever!**
- **Keep your credit report accurate.**

5. Timing Is Everything

At first the credit card company will not work with you. There is a process, a time line that they go through. The credit card companies are trying to get all the money they can as fast as they can. When I first called them and asked if they could lower the interest rates, remove fees or late payments, they said, "No."

When I 'drew a line in the sand,' I knew that I didn't have enough money to pay them and keep up with the other bills, which included a house payment (although I had to eventually sell my house), utilities, and food on the table, so I prioritized what was going to be paid. The credit card companies were near the bottom of the list. When they said they would not work with me, I had to put them on the back burner. I paid the other bills first: housing, food, utilities, etc.

Not making the credit card payments the first month wasn't a big deal. The next month, the statement showed higher interest rates and a late fee. After the second month, when I missed the payment, the phone calls started. I would answer the phone, tell them what was going on, and ask if they would work with me. They would not; many times I would get a reply that they can't do anything until I was five to six months behind. I couldn't pay and the phone calls kept coming. The people on the other end were rude and degrading most of the time. There were times we would let the answering machine pick up the call and let the credit card company leave a message. We told our children not to pick up the phone unless we knew who was calling. We had caller ID, so we could monitor who was calling most of the time. A few times the credit card company would input a local number from the same area code which would throw us off. If we answered the phone, we would talk with the credit card representative and ask them for help. They would not give it; they would want a payment. We couldn't make a payment, so we would tell them that they are on the list.

☛ **KEY:** During the months that no payment is being made is the time to start selling everything unnecessary and stockpiling the cash. See the selling chapter for more information on that.

☛ **KEY:** Once you've missed the first payment and have determined to ride it out, **DO NOT PAY or offer to pay UNTIL the credit card company is willing to settle.** That is, when they are willing to receive a lower payment for the balance due, and they are willing to put it in writing as a settlement.

Be sure it is an actual settlement and not just something the credit card company sends to you.

I have shared these before in the book, but it is important to know the difference between true settlement offers and fake ones. See *Appendix Pages 5-8* for the real ones and *Appendix Page 4* for the false one.

The fake one looks real, but could give you problems later involving extra time, money, and energy and maybe even require hiring a lawyer to straighten the situation out. Don't be fooled.

Continue to sell; continue to stockpile the cash. As time goes on, more phone calls will occur and the credit card companies will be rude, very rude, at times. The good thing is that you can hang up on them. You don't need to talk to them. You don't want to change your phone number, because you want to have some communication with them. Let them know you are still around and wanting to work with them. They will call back every week—maybe every few days, maybe every other day, or even every day. They may even call on Sundays; we had a few that tried that. I was hoping that Sunday would be a quiet day from the phones ringing, but that wasn't always the case.

☛ **KEY:** During the phone calls, a different person from the same department is trying to get more information from you. DON'T give them any new information; always be as general as possible.

Be careful what you say. The credit card company may ask you what you have to sell, or do you have family members that you can borrow money from, or do you have life insurance policy that you can cash in, or an inheritance that you can make payments from, etc.

☛ **KEY:** Don't give them any information. Every time you talk with someone they record it and may be taking notes.

I'll mention this here also, but every time you talk to somebody, and I mean EVERY TIME, it is very, very, very important that you take detailed notes—be very detailed. Something you will need is a telephone recorder. This is a must! You won't believe how many times that having detailed notes and a recorder helped me hold my ground with the credit card companies. Be sure to read more about this in the chapter, Things I Did Right.

If you have caller ID, screen the calls. It is good to talk to somebody once a month. Communication is important and they want to know that you are still available by phone.

The worst period is when you are two to six months behind on your payments. The consistent calls and the credit card representatives make you feel bad. They make you feel lower then dirt. They are trying to tear you down so that you will make an offer to get them off your back. Don't let them tear you down; hold your ground until they are willing to settle and you are able to afford it.

But hang in there, you will get through it. Once you pass the first five to seven months, you will be able to settle with the credit card company. I wrote letters after three months explaining my situation and again asking the credit card company to work with me. I tried to keep the communication open. Usually they would write back and say there is nothing that they could do, but that is part of the process. They won't work with you until they are getting ready to sell the balance to somebody else.

See *Appendix Pages 19-24* for copies of letters that are from one credit card company. Notice the dates. I didn't have the money available to counteroffer, so I had let it run its course. The credit card company did pass it on for their lawyers to take care of it. In December 2009, I did settle with the lawyers for 48% below the requested amount of $19,343. I settled for $10,000. I made a large down payment and then four monthly payments.

☞ **KEY:** It is better for you, and for the credit card company, to come to an agreement instead of the credit card company selling it off; especially if you have done business with them for a long time. You have probably paid that credit card company a lot of interest through the years. Therefore, they could settle a lot easier with you than selling it off to a third party. **If the credit card company can work with you, more than likely they will get more money from you than if they sold the balance to a third party.** Plus it is much better to deal with the original credit card company than a third-party company. From my experience it is harder to deal with the third-party company; they don't have your track record of payments and interest paid. The third party won't settle as quickly or give you as deep of a discount. The third party company, which may be a lawyer, a debt collector, or investment group, paid money for your account so they want to make money off of it; they don't want to write it off. For the original company, if they write it off, there are some tax benefits to them so they may not care as much if the balance is sold. Therefore, it is better to deal with the first company before they sell it to a third-party company.

When negotiating, the credit card company will want to settle or get the account off their books as soon as possible. The sooner they can settle, the better their books look. They want to have a solid commitment on their books. They like lump sum payments, but are willing to take payment plans. The shorter the time frame, the better for the credit card companies, but a person may need more months to pay it off. I was able to settle with some card companies with just one payment, others I made three payments, another one five payments, and one company agreed to a payment plan of forty-eight months. The credit card company wants a solid commitment when you are making payments.

The best time to negotiate is at 5-7 months of non-payment. That is why it is important to stockpile cash during this time. With cash in hand, you have the best negotiating power. If you can do a one-time payment, then do it to get rid of the card.

I mentioned this in an earlier chapter, but it is worth repeating:

I found that the creditors like to have agreements in place by the 24th of the month, although they may give you to the end of the month to postdate a check or get a payment to them.

In my experience, the representative for the credit card company—the person trying to collect the money—has to report to their boss every month. The representative tries to close out as many accounts, or show as many final settlement agreements as possible, by the end of the month. Then, on the first of the month, they start again.

Most representatives hold meetings every Friday morning to update the status of their accounts. They will try to get an answer from you by Thursday evening.

If no progress is being made, they may talk about selling the balance to a third party or about court actions. You don't want the balance to go to court. I know from past experience; I had one credit card company take me to court very quickly. I tried to negotiate with them, but they wouldn't wait for me. Maybe it was because I didn't have any extra money to even start the process. I thought they would have sold it to a third party, but they didn't. The credit card company took it to court and filed a judgment against me. At that point, with the help of a lawyer, I was able to spread the payments out over forty-eight months. I had to pay the whole amount, but even with that, the interest rate was only 8%, which was a lot better than the 27 %. It is always better to negotiate as soon as possible.

NOTE: In summary, Timing Is Everything! While the clock is ticking, especially the first four months, sell everything you can. Once items are sold, stockpile your cash. Then, after the fifth month, start negotiating with the credit card companies. Once you have come to an agreement, follow through with the payments. After the payments are finished, get the letter of satisfaction and keep that document in a file the rest of your life.

⚿ Key Summary:
- **Start selling everything unnecessary and stockpiling the cash.**
- **Once you've missed the first payment and have determined to ride it out, do not pay or offer to pay until the credit card company is willing to settle.**
- **Don't give them any new information; always be as general as possible.**
- **It is better for you, and for the credit card company, to come to an agreement instead of the credit card company selling it off.**

6. Sell, Sell, Sell

This is **KEY**, let me say it again—SELL, SELL, SELL!

I could have done better. Although I started to sell extra items that I had, I didn't do it soon enough.

The key is to prepare for the future. You need to GET READY! Once you stop making payments, the clock is ticking. It is important that you no longer worry about interest rates, late fees, credit scores, etc. Start piling up as much cash as possible so that you will have something to negotiate with. The credit card companies want cash and they would rather settle with some cash instead of writing it off with no cash. Again, they want cash instead of selling the loan for pennies on the dollar to a third party. So get ready!

To get ready, you need to take inventory of everything you can sell. Look for anything that has value. The sooner you sell it (preferably within the first three months of missed payments) the better off you will be. Look around at your inventory. Make a list on paper. Go from room to room, upstairs, downstairs, in the attic, in the shed, in the storage unit, in the garage—wherever you may have items—and put them on the list. Your list may consist of extra tools, extra cars, coins, stamp collections, toys, motorbikes, boats, snow-mobiles, trailers, campers, garage sale items, anything that may sell on E-bay, Craigslist, garage sales, flea markets, etc. The key is to SELL, SELL, SELL. Stockpile the cash. Remember, although you have extra money don't blow it on unnecessary items. You will need the money to negotiate. Don't pay on the credit cards until the credit card companies are ready to settle. Early in the process, I made a mistake by using my savings, my retirement fund, and the children's college fund to pay on the credit cards. It only delayed the problem a couple more months. It would have been better to have saved that money and used it as a payoff settlement.

Selling as many items as you can in the first three months allows you not to feel as panicked as you otherwise would be. This gives you more time so you don't have to sell items at super low prices. Plus, the more cash you have for a reasonable offer, the better off you are and the more likely it is that the credit card company will be willing to settle. They would rather have a one-time payment than many monthly payments. The sooner the credit card company gets the outstanding balance off the books, the better their reporting looks.

☞ Key: Sell EVERYTHING you can! This will help when negotiating.

One of the things I sold was my house. This was very difficult. My wife and I felt a sense of security in owning our own house. I went to the bank to refinance, but the bank was having its own problems like many banks were. They would not loan any money unless a person was within a certain debt-to-income ratio. For the most part, the banks were only loaning money to the people that had money. Because of our debt-to-income ratio, I was not able to get a loan. I had not missed a payment in over twenty years. I had more than 50% equity in the house, but still the bank would not loan the money.

My solution was to sell my house and get it out of my name. I didn't know if there was a lawsuit or judgment coming against me from one of the creditors and if they would be able to put a lien on the house. It cost an extra $2,000 to $3,000, but I felt it was worth it in the long run. By selling the house and getting it out of my name, I removed the danger of losing it. The credit card company couldn't take it if it was no longer mine.

To make things even better, I sold it to somebody I knew who allowed my family to stay in the house. I paid all the utilities, house payments and taxes. This was a friend that was willing to help us out as much as they could. Their debt-to-income ratio was low enough that they could buy the house from my wife and I. Our house became a rental for our friend, which has some advantages to them.

Although it was emotionally hard to sell my house, there were some advantages to it:

1. The house was no longer in my name, therefore I knew the courts couldn't tie it up.
2. I was able to pull out the equity needed to make the settlement payments.
3. It allowed some extra cash for living expenses until we got back on our feet.

As of July 2013, my wife and I have been able to buy back our house from our friend. Since the bad credit problems were sufficiently repaired, the bank was willing to loan us the money. I had been working at the same job for a number of years, which gave us the stability that the bank needed to see. The interest rates were still low, so it worked out well in the end.

As you think of things to sell, put everything on the list—even your house, if necessary. Because of the equity in the house it made sense for us to sell it. We then used that money to negotiate with the credit card companies.

☞ Key Summary:
- **Sell everything you can! This will help when negotiating.**

---

7. Hidden In the Closet

I can't stress enough the importance of detailed note taking and keeping the notes in the file.

I had made a couple of purchases on a business credit card from 2008. I thought it was paid off because I didn't receive any statements concerning an outstanding balance. I must have had a balance of just over $1,000. Somehow the account fell through the cracks, when I had sold my business. I no longer used the account and the account must have gone into a dormant state.

I'm not sure, but when I sold the business, the new owner applied for a company credit card from the same supplier that I used. The new owner also changed the name of the business, but the names were very similar. The business stayed at the same physical location, but had a different post office box. This created confusion with the supplier, causing the supplier to change my mailing address to the new owners address without my permission. Therefore, I no longer received statements or any correspondence.

What I do know is that in 2011, almost three years after I sold the business, I received a phone call saying I owed some money. By this time the balance due had been sold to a third party that was trying to collect anything they could.

I asked the caller for some information about the account. They had trouble answering my questions. Somehow they had my phone number, but they didn't have a lot of information about the history of the account. I didn't know if they had the wrong number or if it really was my account or somebody else's. Maybe the balance due was the new business owners' and they were trying to make me pay for it. Well, after many phone calls, it was verified that it was my bill. I wanted to take care of it but didn't have the money to do that. In Sept. 2011, I came to an agreement with the creditor that I would pay two payments of $275.00 each, one in September and one in October. Once the payments were made, the account would be considered paid in full.

I followed through with my payments, the letter that I received showed that the creditor would accept my two payments as full settlement. See *Appendix Page 25.*

I thought everything was taken care of, only to receive a letter in the mail dated August 2012, stating that I owed $527.57. This came almost one year after the payments were made.

With detailed notes and the settlement letter of agreement, I wrote a letter to the firm that wrote me. One thing I noticed was the letter stating that I still owed the $527.57 was from a different person than the one I'd dealt with almost a year earlier. My guess is that they were subsidiaries of each other so they passed it from one department to another.

After receiving the letter, I wrote them back explaining about the payments made and that the agreement was paid in full according to the settlement agreement. I also mentioned that if there was any other correspondence, they could send it to my address until October 1, 2012. After that they would need to communicate through my lawyer. Then I gave them my lawyer's address. See *Appendix Pages 26-27* for copies of the letters.

Since my letter, I have not heard anything from them. Because I had kept detailed notes and copies of all the important paperwork, I was able to show the creditor that everything was settled as agreed.

You don't know what will show up in the mail, what balances have been sold to third party companies, or if somebody new is going to try and collect money from you. That's why it is important to keep files on every account.

This is a good time to discuss the tax implications and the 1099-C Form. I have mentioned this earlier with more details in the Communication / Negotiation and Follow Through chapter. You may think that you have settled with the credit card company, and you may have the paperwork showing that all payments were made according to the agreement, then come January of the following year, you may get a 1099-C Form. This is a form showing that the credit card company wrote off a certain amount of money and you have to report it on your taxes as income. Therefore, you may owe some income tax on the amount that was written off.

Here is a statement from one of the third-party letters explaining about the 1099-C:

> **Whenever $600.00 or more of debt is forgiven as a result of settling a debt for less than the balance owing, the creditor may be required to report the amount of the debt forgiven to the Internal Revenue Service on a 1099-C form, a copy of which would be mailed to you by the creditor. If you are uncertain of the legal or tax consequences, we encourage you to consult your legal or tax advisor.**

Just be aware that you may receive a 1099-C form. I don't know about you, but I hate surprises. The 1099-C will come by mail in January so you can report it on your tax return. The amount that is sent to you on the 1099-C will also be reported to the IRS. The IRS will cross reference your tax return to make sure you reported it. Depending on the amount that is forgiven by the credit card company, you may owe additional taxes. Therefore, you would want to consult a tax advisor to see if you need to save money in anticipation of additional taxes. See *Appendix Pages 28-31* for some copies of 1099-C.

Remember I mentioned the Capitol One account earlier, and how I finished making payments to them? I received a letter from another creditor about the same account eight months later. Just be aware, some of these accounts may be hiding in the closet for months, if not years.

Many times I have noticed that when an account is sold to a third party, it may go to a lawyer, recovery service, or even an investors group. There were times while I was on the phone, the representative would say, "I need to check with the investors concerning your offer to settle and get back with you." It's not a big deal, but I found it interesting the different groups of people that I dealt with. Some were easier to deal with than others.

☞ **KEY:** This is worth repeating, when dealing with the creditors, you want to deal with the original one before they sell your account to somebody else. I found that I could make better agreements with the original creditors.

Be sure you always have good notes. In the event that a letter comes in the mail saying you owe more money, you will need to have the documentation showing that account has already been paid.

Even as I finish writing this book, I received phone calls from another collection agency that I have never heard of. They are calling my cell phone not knowing who they are calling. When I call them back, I'll program my phone so it blocks caller ID, so they don't know what phone number I am calling from. I'll have the recorder set up so I can record everything they say. They talk so fast, it is hard to understand what is being said. Even though all the creditors have been satisfied, who knows how long these things will be hiding in the closet?

Here is a copy of a letter I received from a fifth party, trying to collect on a debt. See *Appendix 32*. I found it interesting that they admitted saying "the law limits how long you can be sued on a debt. Because of the age of your debt, ... will not sue you for it and ...... will not report it to any credit reporting agency."

But they still tried to get money from me. I sent them a letter explaining the Indiana law of legal theory called "accord and satisfaction." (See *Appendix 13)*. I told them the debt was paid and told them if they had any questions that they could contact my lawyer. I never heard from them again.

⊙━ Key Summary:
- **When dealing with the creditors, you want to deal with the original one before they sell your account to somebody else. I found that I could make better agreements with the original creditors.**

---

8. Just Ask

This may be a short chapter, but very powerful. The concept written about could save a person a lot of money. The title of this chapter is "Just Ask".

It is amazing to me how many people don't ask. As I reflect back in my life, I was raised with my mom saying, "you don't ask". I don't know if it was a pride issue, or maybe she felt embarrassed, I just don't know. But I remember the words, "don't ask". Therefore, if I wanted something, I had to wait until it was offered to me. Sometimes things may have been offered to me and sometimes not.

Without asking for something you may lose out in many ways and miss out on good opportunities. In fact, with the concept of "don't ask" I realized how detrimental that is. For a number of years I had a business that not only included service, but also included sales. I would try and sell new equipment to my customers. I could share the importance of the machines, the benefits, the cost advantage and more, but I always had trouble closing the deal, because I didn't ask for a commitment from the customer. That concept of "don't ask" would follow me wherever I went.

How many situations in life just go on day after day without us asking questions? Maybe we don't think of the right questions to ask or we don't know what words to say, or we think we might be bothering somebody, so we don't say anything.

Well, I want to challenge you to "just ask". If you don't ask, the answer will always be no. But if you do ask you might be surprised with the outcome.

The following are some examples of "JUST ASK":

1. While I was having coffee with a friend, I shared with him about this chapter of "JUST ASK"… I explained how many times we don't ask questions and the reason why we don't ask questions. I shared some stories with him and he admitted that there are times that he wouldn't ask. Later that week, my friend was looking for office space to rent. As he looked at different locations, he came across an office that could work space wise, but the rent was too high. At first he was willing to keep looking without a counter offer. Then he remembered our conversation and the chapter title "JUST ASK." So he thought, I have nothing to lose, so he "ASKED" the landlord of the building if he was willing to lower his price to a certain number. The landlord said he was willing to accept the counter offer. My friend was able to move in at the price he was willing to pay, all because of asking a question. It was a win—win for both parties.

2. At one time, I had a credit card balance of $500 that didn't get paid. That particular month I had paid over $3,000 on the credit card. But because I didn't totally pay it off, I was charged interest of $51.03. At first glance it would appear that I was charged 10% interest in one month because of only having a balance due of $500.

So I called the credit card company and "asked" them about the interest charged and "asked" them if they could reduce the amount. The credit card representative said that they charge on a daily basis of the amount that is on the card, which would accumulate throughout the month. If the balance is paid to zero then the interest fees are removed, but if not paid in full then the card holder is charged whatever the amount of interest has accumulated. In this case $51.03. I asked if they could remove part of the amount, the representative looked at my account and said that they could remove the whole amount and give me credit of the $51.00. They said, "we can do this as a one-time courtesy every 18 months".

Because I asked, I was able to get a $50 credit toward my balance, all because I "ASKED" a question.

⊶ KEY: "Just Ask"

3. I shared the above example with my son, he in turn shared a situation with me. He is working with a web company that was building him the main frame of a web site. My son told me that he had paid a $2,500 deposit that if he went through with the web site, the web site company would credit his account the $2,500 on his overall bill.

As time went on, my son looked at his bills and didn't notice any credit. He thought maybe the web site company just took the $2,500 off the amount owed. He decided to send an e-mail "just asking" about the overall bill, and the $2,500 that was already paid. Within the hour the web site company replied to his question and apologized that they forgot to subtract the $2,500. They said that they would correct the final bill to reflect the lower amount. That was a $2,500 saving just because he "asked a question".

Don't be afraid to ask. Again, if you don't ask, the answer is already no. It doesn't hurt to ask.

4. I witness a situation of a ministry that is supported by donations. The ministry makes a product that is given away free of charge to anyone who would ask. This product is shipped all around the world at no charge. Since the product is given away, the ministry relies on donations to cover the expenses that occur to operate the ministry.

Recently the ministry wrote and submitted a grant proposal "asking" for $20,000 to help cover expenses. The ministry was overwhelmed with joy when they found out that a $20,000 check came in the mail, all because of "asking".

Without submitting the paperwork to the grant and without "asking", the ministry would not have received the $20,000.

5. Here is a cute story of "just asking". I'll change the names to protect members of this certain family. First the back ground: Donna had just lost her grandmother due to a long illness. Donna and her husband Denny had called home to Denny's parents and explained what had happened and the details of the funeral. Denny's parents explained to their grandson Alex, who was 9 years old, that Donna's grandmother had passed away and that it could be a very difficult time for a person as they grieve the lost of a family member.

"Therefore, Alex, when you see or talk to a person that just loss someone, you will need to be very understanding as you approach the subject of someone passing away."

He replied, "okay." The next time Alex spoke to Donna was by text messaging. Alex didn't know how to approach the subject of Donna losing her grandmother, so by text Alex decided to "just ask" a question. The text went as follows: "So any deaths in the family lately?" Donna just laughed, and thought well that's one way to get to the point, "just ask".

6. I am reminded of a time that on a daily basis I would go by a car that was sitting in a yard next to a camper. Months would pass and the car never seemed to move. I decided one day I would try to track down who owned the car and the property it sat on. So I went to the county court house and found the name of the owner. As I looked into it some more, the owner was in a nursing home and the property was being care for by a representative of the owner. I was able to get a hold of the representative so I "ASKED" him if the car was for sale. Now the car wasn't anything to write home about. It did have some rust and had been sitting for a while, but for the right price it might be worth my time. When I asked the representative if the car was for sale, he said "yes". Well, I received a positive answer and I was interested in the car, so I "ASKED", how much? I was surprised at his answer. He said, "well you know the owner is in a nursing home and because of that I can't charge very much, so I will sell it to you for scrap value. If you are interested, I'll take $35 for it and it's yours." I gave him $35, he gave me the title and I towed it to my place. I bought a battery and a set of spark plugs for the car and did a little work to it. I got the car running and drove it around for a number of years.

7. That story reminds me of a time I was visiting a friend. I noticed a car in his driveway, it had some body damage, but seemed to be in decent condition. I "ASKED" what was the story on the car, does it run? My friend said that it was running but the other day it just stopped and he didn't know why. He said he called the junk yard and they were supposed to come and get it the following week and would pay $50 for it. I "ASKED," "is it ok if I look at it?" My friend said "sure go ahead."

I'm not a mechanic, but I do know some basic information about cars. I looked under the hood and after a short time I found a broken wire that went to the starter. I was able to find both ends of the wires and tied them together. At that point I got the key and tried to start it. The car started right up. I "ASKED" my friend if he would take $50 for the car? To my surprise, he said yes! So I bought the car for $50. That car lasted thousands upon thousands of miles. Not a bad deal for "JUST ASKING".

8. My son, was attending college and running on the track team. Because of a track injury, he needed to have surgery on his hip. He was no longer on my insurance, he was on his own. He knew he had insurance through the college, but he never asked if there were any limits to the claim that they would pay out. The surgery was scheduled and preformed. Only later to receive a few invoices from the medical center / doctors, etc. The surgeon's bill was $36,000. The anesthesia bill was $1,000, plus a few smaller bills. Come to find out, the insurance company paid only $25,000. That was their limit to any claims. Wow, what a surprise! What a costly mistake for not asking questions before hand. How in the world can a college student pay

a $11,000 surgeon's bill and $1,000 anesthesia bill? Thankfully, my son started to ask questions. He asked the anesthesia if they would be willing to take payments toward the bill that he owed? They said "Yes, if you can pay $25 per month, we will accept that until it is paid off." So he started paying on that, but what about the other bill? Eleven thousand dollars where will that come from? My son "asked" more questions, only to find out, because he worked part-time for the college as a dorm monitor he was covered under their workman's comp. Which in turned paid the whole amount of $11,000. Although more questions should have been asked at the beginning to find out about pay out limits, etc., at least my son got answers to questions toward the end, which helped immensely.

9. From my own experience, each time we had a hospital bill, we would talk with the billing department and "ask" if they would work with us on a payment plan. Each time they said yes and usually it was without interest.

10. I remember when my wife was pregnant with our first child. Our insurance didn't cover any maternity cost. With that in mind, we went to the doctor's office and "ASKED" if they would be willing to work with us on a reduced payment if we paid cash for the delivery of the baby? They said that if we paid cash, they would reduce the normal cost by 50%. We still had time before the baby was due to arrive, so we were able to save the money to cover the cost of the delivery. All because we "ASKED" a question.

11. Have you ever purchased medicine from the drug store? Well, next time you go and have to pay for the medicine out of pocket, "just ask" if they have that same medicine in a generic form. Also, ask if the generic medicine will do the same thing as the one prescribed. If so, "ask" is the generic medicine any cheaper? More than likely it is.Sometimes it's hundreds of dollars cheaper, all because it's generic.

This has happened a number of times to my daughter. She has allergies that flare up certain times of the year. So the doctor would prescribe the medicine to help fight against the allergies. Many times we have to pay out of pocket, so we would "ask" those questions to the pharmacist. To our surprise we are able to save money.

12. Before GPS, I don't know if you are the type of person that if you were lost you would go to the gas station and ask for directions, or if you would just keep driving hoping that you would find your destination. I'm a person that would pull over and ask. I didn't want to waste my time and gas searching for the place, not knowing if I was going the right way. There were times I would follow the directions the gas station attendant gave me, go down the road a bit, stop again, and ask the same question I did at the last gas station. I wanted to make sure the answers matched and that they were sending me in the right direction. But it was all about "asking". I hope you see the theme of this chapter, "JUST ASK". Without asking the answer is no. There is no harm in gathering information.

Speaking of gathering information, here is a quote I came up with that I have shared with my children, "Ideas cost nothing. Only when you go to implement the ideas is when you need to consider the cost."

Let me explain: Many times we have ideas that may benefit our situation. Those ideas cost nothing. And to make that idea work, you may need to ask questions and gather information. Again, to ask questions and gather information doesn't cost anything. It's when you go to put those ideas or gathered information in motion that you need to consider the cost. Is it worth it or not?

Let me give you an example. A young couple took a job transfer. When they moved to the new location they rented a one bedroom apartment with a one year lease. During their time at this apartment complex, the wife becomes pregnant. Now, as they plan ahead, they think it would be nice to have a two bedroom apartment instead of one. So, that was the idea. But, their thinking was, we signed a one year contract with the apartment complex and there is nothing we can do. Well, my thought is, call the apartment manager and ask, is it possible to switch to a two bedroom apartment if we pay the higher rent without extending our contract? If they don't ask or gather more information the answer is no. But if they ask they may be surprised with the answer. Once all the information is gathered, which cost nothing, then they can consider the cost of the additional expenses to say is it worth it? Do they move or do they stay where they are?

There are many more examples that I could write about, but I hope you get the concept. "JUST ASK", you may be surprised at the answer!

☞ Key Summary:
- **Just Ask.**

9. Inside Information:
Information from a Collection Representative's Point of View

The following is some inside information from a collection representative. A friend of mine was a collection agent for over 14 years, but I did not know that when I was going through my negotiations with the credit card companies. It was only later, a number of years later, that I found out this person was a collection agent. So I spoke with them and asked if they would be willing to answer some questions. They agreed. The following are the answers to my questions. My questions are numbered and italicized, but the answers, from the collection agent, are in bold. A few of the questions have some of my notes, to give additional information. Take time to read through them, there is a lot of helpful information. Keep in mind that this is from the collecting agent's point of view.

1. How important is the communication with the creditor?

It is very important to keep communication open between you and the creditor. That lets the creditor know you want to work with them.

2. From the collector's point of view, what are some of the best things a person in debt can do, who wants to try and work out a plan with the creditor?

Contact the creditor and tell them the situation you are in. That is telling the creditor you are willing to work with them to get the debt paid.

3. What are some things the debtor should not do?
A. Not staying in contact with creditor
B. Not paying what you agreed on with the creditor
C. Not paying on time

4. How important is it for the debtor to keep their address and phone number up to date?

It is very important to keep the creditor up to date with your address and phone number. You don't want the creditor to be looking for you, because they will call your employer and relatives looking for you. The creditor will find you!!! (I have skip traced a lot of people when I was trying to collect from the debtor.)

5. What is Skip Traced?

Skip Tracing is when you don't have an address or phone number for people. You have to find them for the creditor. It takes some research. You get a copy of the application the debtor filled out and see if they have a relative or friend or employer. Then the collection agent starts calling trying to find the debtor. Sometimes collection agent will get a credit report and see what creditors the debtor has and then call them for information. Now with the internet, I'm sure it's easier to find someone because there is so much information about people out there.

Check out <u>fastpeoplesearch.com</u> and see what's being reported about you.

6. What words of advice would you have for someone who wants to work with the collection agency?

It's a scary thing for a person to call a collection agency, but the collection agency is willing to work with you. As soon as you get the notice from the collection agency call them. Just don't ignore the letter, because it's not going away.

Main thing is keep good notes on your conversation with the collection agency. Get name, phone number and extension of the representative. Always write down date of conversation. Remember the representative of the collection agency is taking note of the conversation also.

Author's note: From my experience, the first time I received a notice was after I didn't make a payment. When I contacted the credit card company right away, I asked them if they could help me by lowering the interest rate or removing the late fees. They said they can't do anything until I'm three months or more past due.

I understand the importance of staying in contact with the creditor, but with the credit card companies I had to wait a few months.

Now, this is not the case with a hospital bill, medical center bill or a different creditor. Being up front and open that you can't pay the bill is best. Let the creditor know your situation and try to work out a payment plan.

7. It seemed to me that the collection representative wanted to make progress (have some arrangements in place by Friday or at least something in place over the weekend) Is that the case?

The collection agent's main goal was to get a payment arrangement! Whether it is bi-weekly or monthly, it would depend on the customer and what they could do. If the debtor broke the payment arrangement, the collection agent would either send a letter or call them. The agent usually ended up calling the customer.

8. Will the collection agency take someone to court? If so, how quickly?

Yes, there is no set time frame for taking someone to court. If the creditor sees that the debtor is not willing to pay, that could start legal actions. If the collection agency finds an asset they will take the debtor to court if they are not paying.

9. How does the collection agency find assets and can they garnish a debtor's wages?

Collection Agency can garnish the debtor's wages or seize assets. Assets may include a bank account, car, jewelry, RV, etc. The collection agency does not take the debtors house because the debtor needs someplace to live. How the collection agency finds the asset, the creditor will ask the debtor what they have that might be of value. More than likely the collection agency will just garnish the debtors wages to pay off the debt. (That's what I know of this. I was not involved much with the legal side of things.)

10. What are the time frames of working with the collection agency? And what is the process they go through before they sell the loan to a third party?

The collection agency will attempt to collect the debt voluntary from the debtor, if the collection agency is not able to collect any money, the creditor will sell the note to a 3rd party for a percentage on the dollar.

11. What's the quickest time frame a creditor will sell to a 3rd party, or take somebody to court?

After three months is when a creditor could possibly have the debtor's account sold to a 3rd party or taken to court. Every account is different, it depends if the debtor is willing to work with the creditor. If the creditor sees that the debtor is not willing to work with them, then that's when the creditor may start some kind of action.

Author's note: In my case after the 3rd, sometimes the 4th or even the 5th month, I was able to start negotiations with the credit card companies. I wrote letters to let the creditor know I wanted to work with them. I called the creditor to try and work out a payment plan. The creditor knew I wanted to work with them. There was a time, I told Discover "I have no extra money, although I wanted to work with you, it would be a while until I would be able to save some money." It was soon after that, that I received a notice delivered by the county sheriff that Discover was taking me to court. I don't remember the time frame, (only a few months), but I was very surprised how quickly court actions were taken against me.

12. Will the collection agency take lower payments or be willing to work out a payment plan?

Collection agencies are always willing to work out a payment plan. (I don't remember taking a lower payment when I was collecting). It's a must to keep up with the payments with the collection agency once you make a payment plan.

Author's note: See the beware notes from page 8 concerning the times that the collection agent asked for a higher payment after a six month period. They may have asked me for an extra $10, $20, $25, or $50 per month. I believe one time I was able to give them an extra $10 per month, but the other times I said no I couldn't pay any extra. The collection agent was okay with that, they were just trying to get the note paid off sooner.

13. Does the debtor need to hire a lawyer? If they do, how does that affect the loan and process?

No, it's usually not necessary to hire a lawyer. The only time you would need to hire a lawyer is if you are challenging the debt.

Author's note: I hired a lawyer two different times. The first time was when I made an agreement with the Capital One representative. That person sent me a settlement letter that was a false settlement. The representative didn't write in everything that was agreed to over the phone. (Which at the time, I didn't know it was a false settlement letter.) As I came to the end of the payment plan, my records showed everything was paid according to the agreement. Capital One representative did not agree. I hired a lawyer because I disputed the amount due. With the help of my lawyer, and the laws of Indiana, I did not hear from Capital One again, but Capital One did sell the note to a 3rd party creditor. Once I heard from the 3rd party creditor, I sent them copies of my lawyer's correspondence about the note. I didn't hear from the 3rd party again, but they sold the note to a 4th party creditor. I sent the 4th party creditor copies of my lawyer's correspondence about the note. Once again I didn't hear from the 4th party, but they sold the note to a 5th party creditor. Who also contacted me. No additional payments were made.

The second time I hired a lawyer was when Discover took me to court. I didn't know what to expect, wasn't sure how to handle any negotiations at that time. Therefore, I had my lawyer contact their lawyer to see if a payment plan could be worked out. I was thankful that my lawyer was able to work out a repayment plan over a 48 month period. I did have to pay the full amount I owed Discover, plus interest.

14. Does the debt consolidation companies really work for people to negotiate their balances that are due? Can the debtor get better results if they did the negotiations themselves without going through the consolidation company?

Concerning the consolidation companies do not pay the up-front fees. Get yourself a good licensed credit counselor.

Author's notes: Although I looked into using a consolidation company, I didn't know if I could trust them. After doing some research I found that I was able to get better results then what they could, without their fees. So, I kept control of my accounts and contacted the creditors one by one. See notes on page 12 and 18ff.

15. What would happen when the collection agent is trying to get payment from a debtor, then all of a sudden the debtor said they were working with a consolidation company? How would that change to process of trying to get money from the debtor?

The collection agent would get the name and telephone number of the consolidation company and also the person that the debtor has been talking too. Then the collection agent would call the consolidation company and see how and when the collection agency will be paid.

16. What are some mistakes that people do when dealing with the creditor?
   A. Not keeping in contact with the creditor.
   B. Not sending the payment in on time.
   C. Not sending the payment as they agreed on.

17. What are some of the right things the debtor can do?
   A. Staying in contact with the creditor. (A MUST!!)
   B. Making payment as agreed to.
   C. Making payments on time.

18. What are some things the debtor should or should not say?

Don't say: You are selling something to make the payment and then not send payment.

Don't say: You are borrowing the money from a relative and not make the payment.

My favorite excuse was the cat ate the payment slip so they could not send the payment. That doesn't work!

Do say: You want to make the payment and if you agree on a date you will have the payment sent in a timely matter.

19. If the debtor wants to work with the creditor, is the creditor usually willing to work with them?

YES, the creditor is always willing to work with the debtor. If the creditor is not willing to work with the debtor the creditor will not get paid.

Author's note: The original creditors are who you want to work with. I have found that the original creditors are the ones who will give you the best deal. More than likely you have had an account with them for many years and have paid them a lot of interest throughout those years. Therefore, the creditor has already made some money off of you and can give you better terms.

If the creditor sells the note to a 3rd party, they are only making pennies on the dollar. The 3rd party agency now wants to get all of their money back that they spent on the note, plus more to cover the overhead costs. Therefore, once a 3rd party agency gets the note it is hard to work with them to get good terms. See "KEY" notes on page 28.

20. Can the debtor ask for a different representative to negotiate with? If so, what is the best way to do that?

You can ask for another representative, but why are you asking for another representative? More than likely you are going to hear the same thing that the other representative said.

(In all the years that I was a collector I never had that happen to me). There are good collectors and there are not so nice collectors too. I always tried to be nice because I found out I got better results.

As I wrap up this chapter on *Inside Information*, I asked my friend if they could give some of the excuses why people could not make their payments. Here are some of the replies:

- **My dog or cat ate the payment slip!**
- **Debtor lost the address of collection agency and did not have a stamp to mail the payment!**
- **Heard this a lot – "I was just putting the payment in the mail!"… or… "The check is in the mail!"**
- **A debtor once said… He had to give money to his church.**
- **One guy said… "You can't get blood out of a turnip!"**
- **Heard this one a lot… "Just forgot to make the payment!!"**
- **Some people would do this trick of sending the payment, but would not sign the check! The collection agency had to send it back to the debtor to have the check signed, which would give the debtor more time to put money in**

their account.
- Here's a classic, "We can't pay you because we are going on vacation!!"
- Here is a story I experienced first-hand:

> I was working for a bank in a near-by town and collecting on RVs. There was a debtor that we lost contact with, the bank had no address or phone number. So I started the Skip Tracing process, which is calling his employer and relatives trying to get any information on him that would be helpful. Found out the debtor was working but living on a friend's property with the RV, which was in Kentucky. The friend told me that the Sheriff was looking for the debtor also because of a crime they wanted to talk to him about. The Sheriff called me and told me to stop looking for the debtor because I was getting in the way of the investigation. Since the RV was on the friend's property, the bank had the RV repossessed. The debtor was four months behind on his payments. The sad part was, the RV was in really bad shape when the bank got it back!

You never know what an agent may come across when collecting on bills!

Chapter Summary:
4 Things to keep in mind when working with creditors:
1. Keep good notes of conversation. Get the name and phone number of the person you are talking to and the date of conversation.
2. Keep copies of any correspondence from the creditor and copies of everything you send to the creditor.
3. Keep in contact with creditor!! THIS IS A MUST!! ****(Can't say this enough)
4. Keep payment arrangements as agreed upon!

10. Getting Through It

In this final chapter, I want to thank you for buying this book. I wrote it in hopes that it would be helpful to others. When my wife and I went out for dinner the week of her birthday, we drove a stake in the ground and decided not to live off our credit cards anymore. It was then that I started to look for information that might be helpful to prepare me for what my wife and I would encounter. We knew that we didn't want to file bankruptcy but we didn't know what the upcoming months would look like. I'm assuming that there are more people like me that don't want to file bankruptcy, and want to work with creditors. However, they don't know the best way to do it.

This final chapter will give the greatest comfort of all. People would ask, "How did you get through the difficulty? What was your secret?" I encourage you to read through the whole chapter for the answers. There were days I didn't want to get out of bed. I wanted to hide from society. But all that changed after one night. That night was so special that I had a friend draw a picture of what I saw. To this day, that picture is giving hope and comfort to others that are overwhelmed and struggling. Be sure to see the picture and read the story behind it.

How many times have you heard of couples divorcing and families splitting apart because of financial problems? I want you to know it doesn't have to be that way. In fact, this financial crisis brought my marriage and family closer together.

Problems can be like a wedge. Depending on what side you are on, it will either draw you closer to someone or can separate you and someone.

In our case it brought us closer together. We purposefully said that we will go through this no matter what happens. We may lose everything (which we almost did in the world's eyes), but we will always have each other.

With that being said, we also knew there were some things that would help us get through this difficulty if we applied ourselves.

Some of those things included:

1. Getting together with four to six other couples. We didn't want to be isolated in any way. Although it was difficult to be totally open and honest with others, little by little we were able to share more and more of what we were going through. In turn, this allowed an avenue for the other couples to open up and share the struggles they were going through. I look back and wonder how many couples stayed together and how many families stayed intact all because of being a part of a small group.

This small group was different. Although my wife and I went to church, we didn't feel like we could share our situation with others. Maybe we were fearful what others might think. It seems silly because we should be there to help each other. Instead, we shared with the small group. I remember one day the money was super tight. The food supply was getting low to the point that we didn't have ketchup to have with our meal that my wife was preparing. She prayed and said to the Lord it would be nice to have ketchup with our meal. Later that day there was a knock on the front door; it was somebody from our small group. They had no idea how low we were on groceries, let alone that we were out of ketchup. As my wife and children accepted the groceries, and as they were starting to put them away, they saw that there was a bottle of ketchup in the bag of groceries. We all rejoiced as we thanked the Lord for providing our need that day. This small group was very important.

2. Weekend retreats with friends. Many times, human nature causes us to isolate ourselves from others, but that is the worst thing to do. We need to stay in touch and be involved in the lives of others. Everything we go through has a purpose and that purpose may be to encourage someone else that is struggling. If we isolate ourselves we miss out on a blessing or miss out on being a blessing to somebody else.

3. Listen to Christian radio. As I was going through the tough times, I would listen to Christian radio. Where I am located there are a couple of Christian radio stations that play just Christian music. I found there were messages in the songs the artists were singing. Those messages were very comforting. I would also listen to thirty-minute programs that would give encouraging messages from the Bible. It was amazing how many times a message would hit close to my situation. Frequently, I found comfort and peace that would help me get through another day. I encourage you to tune in to Christian radio stations in your area or on the internet or even order some messages on CD or get some books that might be helpful.

4. Read Christian books. There were two books that helped me the most during this time. One was *The Bible*, our road map of life from God; just reading it helped. The other was *The Red Sea Rules*, written by Robert Morgan. These books were very, very helpful. I didn't feel like a failure, I knew there were no surprises to God. God knew right where I was and He had a plan for me, even in the midst of the huge trial I was going through.

The neat thing about *The Red Sea Rules* was that it gave some practical ideas that were helpful. In fact, above the title it says, *10 God–given strategies for difficult times.* This is a small book that is quick and easy to read. I suggest you buy the book and read it. Not only will it help you, you can then pass it on to somebody else to help.

As I read the book, *The Red Sea Rules*, one of the things that spoke to me was to **Trust God**. Trust God in ALL circumstances. One of the chapters is titled, "Trust God to Deliver in His Own Unique Way." As I look back over the situation, it was God that delivered me from the bondage of the creditors. It was God that allowed the items I had for sale to sell at a good price so I could pay the creditors. It was God that allowed me to find favor in the creditors eyes so that I could settle for 50% to 80% lower than the balance due on some of the credit card debt. It was God that provided the money needed to make the final payments. I didn't need to trust in myself and my own abilities of what I could do, but I needed to trust God and the way that He would deliver me out of this situation.

5. Pray. While reading God's word, I would also spend time praying. I would pray by myself a lot, but there were times when I would pray with my wife. Those times became very precious. When we prayed together, it gave my wife the security that I couldn't give. There was a peace that was beyond words, a security that my wife needed, because it seemed like our world was falling apart; which, in reality, it was because we had lost our savings, our kids' college funds, our retirement accounts, our coin collection, and other items that we had sold, including our house. Our world was falling apart, but through prayer with one another there was comfort.

There was peace and comfort through prayer and reading God's word. There was a peace of knowing that God is in control of all things and that there were no surprises in Him. I knew that I could trust Him in every circumstance, including this one. If it meant losing almost everything, I could trust Him. I knew from the Bible there are promises God makes. If He makes those promises, He will keep them. One of the promises that I hung on to was that He would never leave me nor forsake me. Although there may be times that I felt alone, I knew I never was. God would see me through.

In the midst of all the phone calls, with the creditors calling day after day, the emotional drain was very difficult; the stress was so bad that it started to affect my speech and my thinking. It was difficult to wake up to another day because I didn't feel like getting out of bed. I wanted to hide from society, but I knew that I had to keep going, keep moving forward, even though some days I felt like I was going backwards. One night while I was sleeping, I had what appeared to be a dream. A lot of times I don't remember dreams, but this one I did.

In this dream, I was moving forward, I was walking down a path. I looked around and saw what appeared to be a war zone. Total devastation was all around me, trees were uprooted, buildings were crumbled, and craters covered the landscape from bombs exploding. At that same time, the enemy fire was continually coming at me and trying to destroy me from every angle.

As I walked, my Lord Jesus was with me. He was walking alongside me on the path. But as we walked, we were encased in a bubble. The bubble was so strong that the darts and the weapons of the enemy could not penetrate the bubble.

The Lord and I walked inside the bubble. It was quiet and peaceful—a sweet time of talking and discussing life's concerns. Anything that was going on outside the bubble couldn't be heard. The Lord impressed on my heart, saying to me, **"I won't remove you from the war zone, but I will protect you from the enemy. As we walk this journey together, I will always be with you and we will have a sweet time of fellowship each and every day. Trust Me as I see you through."**

As I woke up that morning, I knew that I had received a promise from the Lord. This was a promise that I could take with me on the rest of this journey. No matter what comes in front of me, I knew God would be with me and see me through to the end. This was very encouraging. Although my circumstance didn't change, my hope did. For God said that He wouldn't remove me from the "war" or "so-called creditors," but He would see me through. That was a promise I could hold on to.

At the time of this writing it has been almost five years walking through this, but it has been a time of drawing closer to God and trusting Him in everything. As I mentioned earlier, this difficulty, this financial crisis, was a wedge. Was it going to push me away from people, including my wife and family, and away from God? Or was it going to draw me

The Lord is on my side; I will not fear
What can man do to me? Ps 118:6

I Peter 4:12 "Dear friends, do not be surprised at the painful trial you are suffering, as though something strange were happening to you."

closer to people, my wife, my family, and to God? I purposed to have it draw me closer to God and others.

Let me ask you, what is the enemy trying to destroy you with? Is it fear, doubt, a loss of job, not enough income, sickness, cancer, divorce, wayward children, creditors calling, foreclosure, losing your home, losing your retirement, loss of a family member, or (fill in the blank) _____?

You may be in the same boat that I was in, or you may know somebody that is. I hope that you find comfort and peace in this book by realizing that there is HOPE no matter what life circumstances may bring your way.

The greatest thing is that God has told us His story through His word, the Bible, and that we can be a part of that story. He wants us to draw near to Him and He wants to draw near to us. James 4:8a says:

> Draw near to God and He will draw near to you.

In His Word, God has told us that through Jesus Christ, His Son, we are offered eternal life. A life that will allow us to be forever with Him. Even after we pass away from this earth, for this earth is only temporal, we can be with God forever. In the New Testament in John 14:6, Jesus has said,

> "I am the Way, the Truth and the Life. No man comes to the Father except through Me."

It was Jesus Christ that gave His life by dying on the cross for me and my wrongdoings and for you and your wrongdoings. He died, was buried, and rose again to show that He has power over death. I Corinthians 15:3–4 says:

> For I delivered to you first of all that which I also received: that Christ died for our sins according to the Scriptures, and that He was buried, and that He rose again the third day according to the Scriptures.

And because of that He can offer us eternal life, power over death, if we come to Him and accept His work on the cross in our place. The price has already been paid for you and for me.

God's Word tells us that if anyone calls on the name of Jesus, they will be saved. Romans 10:9-10, says,

> That if you confess with your mouth Jesus as Lord and believe in your heart that God raised Him from the dead, you shall be saved: for with the heart man believes, resulting in righteousness, and with the mouth he confesses, resulting in salvation.

This is the HOPE that we have, the HOPE that we have been offered. This is the True HOPE that helps me get through another day. This is the HOPE of life forever. This is the HOPE that I want to share with you. May you also find the True Hope of Eternal Life with God!

I believe this is the reason that I went through all of this, so that I can share these words of encouragement with others.

People have asked me, "Where are you and your family today? Did this financial nightmare take you down, destroy you, and put you under? Or, were you able to bounce back?"

I decided to write a brief summary of where we are right now. Although life seemed hopeless as I went through the financial nightmare, each day wondering when will it be over? How long will it take to get through the struggle? Will life ever by different? Will life be better?

Well, with the financial struggle behind me, I can truly say that life is much better. It is better for my wife and me because we allowed this circumstance to pull us together, instead of apart. We have used our experience to help others that are going through similar difficulties. And most important, we allowed this circumstance to draw us closer to the Lord. I have also been able to share in churches about our struggles, which allowed me to encourage others.

One of the highlights of perseverance is that my wife and I were able to buy back our house from our friend. That was a big praise, because it gave my wife the much needed security again.

As for our children: three of them have graduated from college, two of them are currently in college, and the youngest child is planning on attending college this fall. Each of the children was able to get scholarships that helped cover the expenses. As I was going through the financial difficult, I wondered if any of them would be able to attend a college of their choice. Sure enough, they did!

Two of the children are married, each with a child. So being a grandparent is a new joy for my wife and me to experience. Spoil the grandchildren and send them home, right? What a joy!

One of the children is engaged to be married this year. So we are in the process of planning a wedding and a time of celebration.

One of our children worked with the airlines. Because of the benefits, my wife and I were able to fly to various places at a low cost. One of those places was Hawaii. What a beautiful place to visit.

I am able to work with a ministry that allows me to use my gifts and talents for God. Going to work isn't a job, it is a privilege knowing that the things I do can impact lives for eternity.

I know there is purpose in everything I do. That is what I want to leave with you. Life is worth living, don't give up. Even if you are in the midst of the struggle, you will get through it. Things will get better. You will be able to enjoy life again. There is hope!

If you have questions about this HOPE or want more free information, please contact me at:

Finding Freedom From Debt, LLC
P.O. Box 4, Bremen, IN 46506

I can also be reached at:
www.findingfreedomfromdebt.com

If this book has been of help to you, please write and tell me how you have been encouraged. Don't go through this struggle alone. May you find comfort and peace in God who created you and loves you.

One final thought, something to meditate on:

No God—No Peace
Know God—Know Peace

Blessings to you. Thank you for buying this book, I hope you have found it very helpful.

Appendix Page 1
Conversation with Credit Card Representative

The following is in reference to   Credit card.

This is listed under   A statement on May 9,
2009 it shows a balance of $8,789.90. Around Aug. 1, 2009 they said I owe approx.
$9010.00

On July 31, 2009 I spoke with supervisor   (I think it's spelled that way)
at   he told me he could settle for $4,598.00 paid over a 5 months.

I told him I would call back next week. I called back Aug 3 and again on Aug 10.

I spoke with Mr.   as a representive, he said he would accept an
agreement with a settlement ceiling of $4591.00. He said I would need to pay $1,500
down and $200 per month after that. (with a max of 23 months) but he said to make final
payment arragements on the 15 month. Again he stressed that it would be a ceiling of
$4,591.00. All payments made would go toward the ceiling amount.

There were two conversations, the first was 18 minutes in lenght, the second was shorter,
placed around 4:30 pm. of Aug 10, 2009

On 8-10-2009 at 4:54pm they faxed me a paper showing the payment plan, signed by

I gave them permission to withdraw the money from   First
withdraw would be $1,500 on Aug 12, 2009 and $200 / month on the 15 of every month.

I made payments $200 / month every month as mentioned. I called on Oct 7,2010, at
10:10 am I spoke with Mr.   to make the final payment arrangement of
$291, (around the 15th month as he requested) he said the payoff balance was $6823.64.
I mentioned about the ceiling, all payments applied toward the cap. He put me on hold, to
listen to the agreement, he heard the agreement, but needed mangers final approval, he
said he would call back in about 1 hour. (phone time was approx. 12 min.)

The manager,   called me back and said he listened to the conversation
and said it was an agreement but not a settlement. And that I stilled owed the money. He
said sorry for the miscommunication.

After the $1,500 down payment on Aug 12, 2009 the amount owed would be $3,091.00.

As of Nov. 1, 2010 final payment would be $291.00, after the 15th of Nov. the final
payment would be $91.00.

Appendix Page 2
Conversation with Credit Card Representative

I called on Dec. 2, 2010, Spoke with Mr.   concerning the arrangements we had made eariler in 2009 and told him I was calling back as he requested before the end of the settlement. He put he on hold, then   manager, came on and said "I remember talking with you, but sorry for the miscommunication, no settlement was made. He did say that the recorded conversation was on record and I had ask to here it so we were on the same page. He put me on hold (this called started around 11:25 am.)

The recording that Mr.   played cut into the conversation (didn't play the beginning of it) and it only talked about 23 months max. of $200.00 per month. Mr.   said he would need upper management to reveiw the tape and pull the archives and that I could call back Fri. Dec. 3 at 11 am EST will be best. (this is on my tape first side 00-1001)

I called Dec. 3 at 11:30 am est. tried to talk with   he was in a meeting with his manager, they put me to his voice mail. I said I would call back. I called back at 12:00 est. spoke with   he said there was no recordings, so I mentioned the dates of July 31, 2009, Aug. 3,2009, Aug. 10, 2009. He heisated put me on hold and came back and said there was no recordings. I asked him about the agreement vs a settlement.................

Tape, second side 00-464, 12-3-10

I sent a check on Dec. 3, 2010 for the amount of $91.00. (have a photo copy of it)

The following is to be applied to account #   under the name of

"This is a payment toward the said agreement made with   on August 10, 2009. Cashing of this check verifies the said arrangement that this is the final payment and no additional payment is needed for said account."

Valid until Dec. 31, 2010 $91.00 by Dec. 15th   ck #

Sent the check to their location, they sent it back as unable to cash. They would not accept as final payment. They continued to take out of my checking $200.00 per month.

July 8, 2011 Meet with the laywer,   and present my case that has not held up to their agreement as on the recording (which they have, and I only have a part of it, they didn't play it all back to me), concerning the ceiling of $4,591.00 and the Indiana state law of "accord and satisfaction", and see about getting a refund for the additional amount that they took out of my account. After meeting with   he suggested that I close out the account so they can not take any more $ out. He also said it is not best to sue them, but wait till they sue you then do a counter sue and request the

Appendix Page 3
Conversation with Credit Card Representative

courts to get the recordings. To sue them you have to go to their location. (let them come to you.)

July 15,2011 Mr   called and was wanting more money. I told him I would call him back next week.

July 20, 2011 9:35 am est on the tape 00-87 I called and spoke with   told him that the call was being recorded. When I called him back, he complimented me by saying "your a man of your word." I told him that the state of Indiana says any agreemnet made is a binding contract, therefore I have fulfill my end of it". He would not speak any more on that but said I would need to talk to   and that he would call me.

July 26, 2011 I received a phone call from   She mentioned the settlement of 50%, and was trying to read some of the notes. She gave me her hours for the next 3 days and I told her I would call back. Tues left in the afternoon, Wed. Thurs 11 am - 9 pm CST.

July, 27, 2011 I called approx 8:15 pm spoke with   I told her the call was being recorded on my end. Tape 00- 136. She was a middle person trying to read the notes and that she never heard of Mr.   although she has worked there 7 years. She had trouble reading the notes because of the misspellings and they were not in order. So I explained to her the agreement that was made, the final payment I tried to make, but it was returned and that after doing the math, I overpaid $1509 that I would like a refund. She said that she would write down the account number and that she would pass it on to somebody else, because she was only a middle person. She also said that they would probably call next Tues.

Notice the notes that were taken:

Date, time, who I spoke with, summary of the conversation, action taken, or to be taken.

It appeared from later conversations with the creditors that I took better notes than they did.

Appendix Page 4
False Settlement Letter

Address Service Requested

August 10, 2009

| Creditor: Capital One Bank (USA), N.A. |
| Account No: |
| URS No: |
| Amount Due: $9181.07 |
| Telephone: |

Dear

This notice is to confirm we have recorded your permission to create and deposit the following check reproductions on the dates indicated. Please review the checking information for accuracy.

Checking account of

Bank name:
Routing number. Account number:

Check No	Check Date	Amount	Check No	Check Date	Amount
9000	08/12/2009	$1500.00	9001 *Paid*	09/15/2009	$200.00
9002 *Paid*	10/15/2009	$200.00	9003	11/15/2009	$200.00
9004	12/15/2009	$200.00	9005	01/15/2010	$200.00
9006	02/15/2010	$200.00	9007	03/15/2010	$200.00
9008	04/15/2010	$200.00	9009	05/15/2010	$200.00

and additional checks agreed to but not listed here due to space.

MAX. 24 month But must PAY OFF EARLY BY Month 15

Please destroy the original checks and enter the transactions in your check register. If you have any questions, please call

This communication is from a debt collector. We are required to inform you that this is an attempt to collect a debt, and any information obtained will be used for this purpose.

Sincerely,

| Creditor: Capital One Bank (USA), N.A. |
| Account No: |
| URS No: |
| Amount Due: $9181.07 |
| Telephone: |

You May Call Our Office 24 Hours A Day

From my notes: A quote from the representative: "The maximum amount you need to pay is $4,591.00, all payments are applied toward the loan. Maximum amount of time is 24 months." Spoken on 8/10/09. His first conversation was 18 minutes, and second conversation was at 4:30pm EST.

Appendix Page 5
Valid Settlement Letters: From Credit Card Company A

January 8, 2009

RE: Your Visa account ending
Balance: $18,187.44

will accept $3,700.00 as settlement in full on the above account due by June 15, 2009. Or this can be done in 3 monthly payments of $1,233.00 each. The first payment of $1,233.00 must be received no later than June 15, 2009, the second payment of $1,233.00 must be received by July 15, 2009, the third and final payment of $1,234.00 by August 14, 2009. As long as these payments are here on the agreed upon dates this account will be considered settled in full.

Upon receipt and clearance of the payment, we will report the account as settled for less than the full balance & amount owed will be ($0.00) zero. A 1099-C form will be produced and sent to the Internal Revenue Service as mandated by the IRS, if the forgiven balance is $600.00 or greater. The payments should be guaranteed overnight mailed to or sent to my attention at:

If you have any questions or would like to make these payments over the phone, contact me toll free at   Our office hours are Monday through Friday 8:00 A.M. to 5:00 P.M. Central Standard Time.

Sincerely,

I accepted on 5/18/09 and made three monthly payments.

Pre-Legal Department

Appendix Page 6
Valid Settlement Letters: From Credit Card Company B

June 08, 2009
ACCOUNT   0000000

Current Outstanding Balance: $16,608.79
Settlement Amount: $2000.00

Dear

This letter is to confirm that   has received the final owed
pursuant to the settlement agreement you entered into in connection with
the above referenced account. The account is now considered settled.

If payment is rejected for any reason   agreement to
accept less than the current balance owed on the account is terminated and
the account owner will be responsible for payment of the current balance.

If the settlement resulted in debt forgiveness of an amount equal to or
greater than $600.00, the Internal Revenue Service ("IRS") requires
             to report the amount of the forgiveness of debt to the
IRS.   will comply with that IRS requirement. You may be
required to include the amount of the debt forgiven as income on your
federal income tax return. Please consult your tax advisor or other
qualified person regarding this matter.

If you have any questions concerning this matter please contact

Sincerely,

Business Card Collections

Once final payment is made, keep in a file forever, so they don't come back and say you owe more money.

Be sure to get a Satisfaction Letter of Paid in Full.

Appendix Page 7
Valid Settlement Letters: From Credit Card Company C

May 11, 2009

                              (Business)
              (Guarantor)
              (Cardholder)

FAX

Account No.   55
Account Balance: **$ 18,129.46**

Dear

Per our conversation, this letter sets forth a ***proposal to
settle*** the above-referenced account pending final approval.
We will accept **$2,000.00** as a settlement on this account. To
accept this offer, you must agree to the following payment
schedule:

PAYMENT DATE   **AMOUNT**   **CONFIRMATION #**

5/14/2009 $2000.00   BRANCH PAYMENT

PLEASE CALL TO CONFIRM BRANCH PAYMENT

By completing this payment plan, your account will be
considered settled, and you will **not** be obligated to pay the
remaining balance, provided no additional charges appear on
this account after the date of this letter. Also, any future
account activity that results in a credit balance will
become the property of

Any violation of this agreement will result in the full
balance of **$ 18,129.46** being due immediately. All payments
must be received by the above stated due date.

For your convenience, you can make your payment over
the telephone by contacting one of our knowledgeable Account
Managers at   Monday through
Thursday 8 a.m. to 8 pm. and Friday 8 a.m. through 5 p.m.

Sincerely,

Senior Customer Service Advocate

A valid Settlement Letter.

**I made the payment of $2,000, then
received a settlement letter on 08/08/09**

Appendix Page 8
Valid Settlement Letters: From Credit Card Company D

Date: July 30, 2009
You Owe:
Balance Due: $27,077.37
Account #:
File #:

Dear

In an effort to assist you in resolving your account, our client has authorized us to offer you the opportunity to settle your account. This means instead of paying the full balance due on your account, you can pay **30.000%** of the total amount due and the above-mentioned client will consider this account settled.

[handwritten: PAID 8/20]

This is a great opportunity to finally take care of this long overdue account. If you wish to take advantage of this one-time offer, contact our office or mail your remittance in the form of a cashier's check or money order in the amount of $1,353.87 due by 7/31/09; $1,353.87 due by 8/31/09; $1,353.87 due by 10/30/09; $1,353.87 due by 11/30/09; $1,353.87 due by 12/31/09 If the settlement amount is not received within 1 days of the date of this letter, this offer will become null and void.

[handwritten: PAID 7/30]

[handwritten: MONEY WAS CREDITED TO ACCOUNT]

[handwritten: From Payment Due Jan 2010]

does not report any information to any credit bureaus or agencies.

We are being as flexible as possible with you so call us today and let us help you resolve this overdue account. However, if you dispute this account or any portion thereof, please refer to the reverse side of this letter for an explanation of your rights.

> I made the six payments then received a settlement letter. This letter was interesting because when the credit card company wrote it, they forgot to put in the September payment. The nice thing was I made the final payment in January 2010, which allowed the 1099-C to be issued for the 2010 tax period. This offset a lot of money away from the 2009 taxes, but taxes were due with the 2010 tax return.

Appendix Page 9
Letter from 3rd Party Lawyer & My Lawyer's Correspondence

ATTORNEYS AT LAW

October 11, 2011

PLEASE REFER TO OUR FILE NO.

Re: Your indebtedness to: Bank (USA), N.A., FORMERLY KNOWN AS   BANK

As of the date of this letter, you owe $5,704.81. Because of interest, late charges, and other charges that may vary from day to day, the amount due on the day you pay may be greater. Hence, if you pay the amount shown above, an adjustment may be necessary after we receive your check, in which event we will inform you before depositing the check for collection. For further information, write the undersigned or call either

Dear

** This communication is from a debt collector and this is an attempt to collect a debt and any information obtained will be used for that purpose.***

Unless you dispute this debt, or any portion of it, within 30 days after you receive this notice, we will assume that it is valid.

If you notify us in writing within the 30 day period that you dispute this debt or any portion of it, we will obtain verification of the debt or a copy of any judgment and mail it to you.

If the above creditor is not your original creditor and you submit a written request within the 30 day period for the name and address of the original creditor, we will supply such information to you.

If you do dispute this debt or any portion thereof, in writing in the 30 day period, or if you within the 30 day period request the name and address of the original creditor, we will cease collection of the debt or any disputed portion thereof until we mail you verification of the debt or a copy of any judgment or the name and address of the orginal creditor.

Very truly yours.

This is a letter from the 3rd Party lawyer that I received after I paid the amount agreed on. This lawyer bought the note from the credit card company then tried to come after me for more money. So I had my lawyer write a letter back.

See Appedix 10

Appendix Page 10
Letter from 3rd Party Lawyer & My Lawyer's Correspondence

Attorneys at Law

November 7, 2011

Please Reply To:

RE: Bank vs.   – Your file #

Dear

Please be advised that I represent Mr.   with respect to an amount your client is claiming due from him. Mr.   has kept meticulous records of his negotiations with the various collection agencies that have contacted him about this debt. I thought the easiest thing for me to do was just to include herewith a copy of the letter that Mr.   sent me recently, setting out a history of his account from his perspective. There are actually two letters that I am enclosing with the most recent one being an updated version.

In any event, Mr.   thought that he had reached an agreement, whereby if he paid a sum certain, this account would be satisfied. In consideration of that agreement, he made certain payments as detailed in his letters. Now, it appears that this collection has been turned over to your office instead and maybe you are not aware of the agreement that Mr.   had with

In any event, I would appreciate it if you could review his information with your client(s) and determine whether this case can now be dismissed, based on the earlier agreement reached with Mr.   and the payments he has already made.

I look forward to hearing back from you on this. Thank you for your attention hereto.

Yours truly,

This is a letter sent to their lawyer from my lawyer. I did not hear from him again, but the note was sold, again, to another party that tried to collect more money from me.

Appendix Page 11
Subsidiaries of Same Parent Company

PRIVACY NOTICE

This Privacy Notice is being given on behalf of each of the following related companies (the "Sherman Companies"). It describes the general policy of the Sherman Companies regarding the personal information of customers and former customers.

Sherman Acquisition Limited Partnership	Resurgent Capital Services L.P.	Anson Street LLC
Sherman Acquisition II Limited Partnership	Resurgent Capital Services PR LLC	Ashley Funding Services LLC
Sherman Acquisition L.L.C.	LVNV Funding, LLC	Credit One Bank. N.A.
Sherman Acquisition TA LP	Ascent Card Services, LLC	SFG REO, LLC
	Ascent Card Services II LLC	PYOD LLC
		Tradd Street LLC

Information We May Collect. The Sherman Companies may collect the following personal information: (1) information that we receive from your account file at the time we purchase or begin to service your account, such as your name, address, social security number, and assets; (2) information that you may give us through discussion with you, or that we may obtain through your transactions with us, such as your income and payment history; (3) information that we receive from consumer reporting agencies, such as your creditworthiness and credit history, and (4) information that we obtain from other third party information providers, such as public records and databases that contain publicly available data about you, such as bankruptcy and mortgage filings. All of the personal information that we collect is referred to in this notice as "collected information".

Confidentiality and Security of Collected Information. At the Sherman Companies, we restrict access to collected information about you to individuals who need to know such collected information in order to perform services in connection with your account. We maintain physical safeguards (like restricted access), electronic safeguards (like encryption and password protection), and procedural safeguards (such as authentication procedures) to protect collected information about you.

Sharing Collected Information with Affiliates and Third Parties

Sharing with Affiliates. From time to time, the Sherman Companies may share collected information about customers and former customers with each other and with their affiliated financial services companies in connection with administering and collecting accounts.

Sharing with Third Parties. The Sherman Companies do not share collected information about customers or former customers with third parties, except as permitted by applicable privacy law. For example, collected information may be shared in certain circumstances (A) with third parties, to service or enforce accounts, (B) with credit reporting agencies, and (C) with law enforcement officials, to protect against fraud or other crimes.

Special Notice Regarding Collected Information Subject to the Fair Debt Collection Practices Act.

This Privacy Notice is being sent to you by the Sherman Companies in accordance with federal privacy law, and it describes our privacy practices generally. However, please be assured that collected information that is received or used for purposes of collecting a debt subject to the Fair Debt Collection Practices Act is communicated only in accordance with that Act.

There are 15 different names listed under the "Sherman Companies"

Appendix Page 12
Satisfaction and Release of Judgment Letter

STATE OF INDIANA) IN THE   CIRCUIT COURT
)SS:
COUNTY OF   ) CAUSE NO.

)
)
)
)
)
)
)
)
)
)
)
)
        Defendant   )

                SATISFACTION AND RELEASE

                    OF JUDGMENT

Comes now the Plaintiff and having received full satisfaction,

now releases the Judgment entered herein against the Defendant

                            Respectfully,

This is a copy of the Satisfaction and Release
of Judgment, once all payments were made
concerning the lawsuit.

Keep on file the rest of your life!

Appendix Page 13
Letter of "Law of Legal Theory"

— Attorneys at Law —

October 28, 2010

Please Reply To:

Dear

Sorry it has taken me a while to get back to you on your letter. Indiana has a legal theory called "accord and satisfaction". This theory says that if parties reach an agreement on how an account is to be paid and the paying party completes the terms of that agreement, the account is satisfied, even if the payment was not made in full.

However, if you can prove that the arrangements were made as you indicated in your letter, I think a court would find that an accord and satisfaction had occurred, so that you did not have to pay the balance of the account that they apparently are still claiming. Unfortunately, the only way to present this theory would be to file suit against them for a declaratory judgment or wait until they sue you for the balance and then use the accord and satisfaction as an affirmative defense.

Another option might be for me to write a letter to them indicating that we believe an accord and satisfaction had occurred, regardless of what they understood in hopes that they might then write the balance of the account off.

Feel free to contact my office and schedule an appointment to come in and discuss that possibility if you would like to pursue that. Feel free to contact me also if you have any questions on anything.

Yours truly,

This is a letter from my lawyer to me explaining the law about "Accord and Satisfaction." My lawyer felt it would hold up in court, but it never went to court. The third party lawyer ended up selling the note to a fourth party collector.

Appendix Page 14
Letter from 4th Party Collector & My Correspondence

RE: Your account with

For/Original Creditor:
Current Creditor:
Account Number: ***********
Current Balance: $2898.83

Office Hours (Eastern Time):

Monday - Thursday	8:00 am - 9:00 pm
Friday	8:00 am - 8:00 pm
Saturday	8:00 am - 2:00 pm
Sunday	Closed

Reference No.
Date: 07/04/2012

- - - - - - - - - - - - - - - - PLEASE DETACH AND RETURN THIS PORTION WITH YOUR PAYMENT - - - - - - - - - - - - - -

has purchased the above-referenced account from the original creditor and has authorized   to initiate collection efforts to recover the total amount due as noted above. Please be advised that if we are unable to come to terms on a repayment agreement,   may forward your account to a lawyer to review for potential legal action.

Please send your payments to:
Don't forget to include your reference number and make your check payable to   You can also make this payment online by visiting www   com. You will need your reference number and PIN from the bottom of this letter to pay online.

Sincerely,

Phone Number: 1-866

This is an attempt to collect a debt and any information obtained will be used for that purpose. This is a communication from a debt collector.

Unless you notify this office within 30 days after receiving this notice that you dispute the validity of the debt or any portion thereof, this office will assume this debt is valid. If you notify this office in writing within 30 days after receiving this notice that you dispute the validity of this debt or any portion thereof, this office will obtain verification of the debt or obtain a copy of a judgment and mail you a copy of such judgment or verification. If you request this office in writing within 30 days after receiving this notice, this office will provide you with the name and address of the original creditor, if different from the current creditor.

This is a letter from the fourth party collector trying to get money from me. I sent them a response letter and never heard from them again

Appendix Page 15
Letter from 4th Party Collector & My Correspondence

July 18, 2012

The following is in reference to a letter I received with a reference No. 1

From reading the letter it seems that you have acquired an old debt that has been settled according to the terms that were agreed on.

I wish   would have been more honest with you concerning this. The debt has been paid off according to the agreement that was set by both parties on August 10, 2009. The terms were as follows: On August 12, 2009 a down payment of $1,500 would be made, along with a monthly payment plan of $200 per month until a cap of $4,591.00 is reached. The representative from Capital One,   told me on a recorded line that all payments will go toward the debt with an agreed upon cap of $4,591.00. With that agreement in place, I made the $1,500 down payment then made every monthly payment until July 15, 2011. By mistake I ended up overpaying the debt by $1,509.   kept taking money out of my account from Dec. 15, 2010 to July 15, 2011.)

Enclosed please find a copy of the agreed arrangement, alone with a paid payment schedule of every payment.

I wish   or whoever you bought it from would have been upfront and honest with you. If you have any questions, you may contact me by mail only, till Sept. 1, 2012. After that date you will need to contact my attorney for any additional information. He can be reached at:

Sincerely,

This is my letter to the fourth party collector; never heard from them again. But they seem to sell the balance to somebody else because I received another notice.

Appendix Page 16
Explanation Letter to Credit Card Companies

Dear _____   April 23, 2009

Please allow me a few minutes of your time. I am writing in reference to my account, # _____   I do recognize that I owe you money.

Over the last 15 years I have had good credit and have been able to make payments, that is, until Nov. 2008. Being self employed, the economy took a toll on my business, we live in an area where the unemployment rate is over 15%. I went to the bank and tried to get a loan, but the bank had tightend their lending rules and I was not able to get one.

My wife and I have seven children, all at home. Four of them have been adopted from Haiti. We have shared our life with them and given them a home. If they were still in Haiti they may not have survived. (Please see enclosed photo.)

Because of the added loss of income, we can no longer make our payment. We have been reduced to keeping food on our table, a roof over our head, and clothes on our back. Our income is approx. $29,000 per year, we have a mortgage payment of $810.00, which we are paying to keep from foreclosure. We are thankful we have no van payments, (one van is 1994 and the other is 1996), we've never had cable TV, don't take vactions and live on a very tight budget. The rest of the money goes to food and utilities.

Due to our desperate situation, I am not able to make any payments at this time. I am asking if you could show kindness, grace and mercy to us, by forgiving our debt. If you can we would be forever greatful. If not, I am willing to make arrangements to pay you back, but it may be 9-12 months before I get back on track to make small monthly payments.

I can be reached by mail at:

I am sincerely sorry that I am not able to pay at this time.

Thank you for your time,

Very early on, this is the letter I wrote to the credit card companies explaining why I could not pay, but wanted them to know I was willing to work with them.

Appendix Page 17
Western Union Payment Form

PAYMENT via Quick Collect®

WESTERN UNION

Western Union® Gold Card or phone number
Número de Tarjeta Dorada de Western Union® o teléfono
_____ OR (_____)

Agent Use Only
Sólo Para Uso del Agente
Money Transfer Control Number

1 Payment Information

Dollar Amount/Cantidad en Dólares
$ _____

Company Name/Nombre de la Compañía

Pay to/Páguese a: _____

Code City/Código de Ciudad: _____

Attention/Atención: _____

Promo Code/Código de Promoción: _____

2 Sender Information

First Name/Primer Nombre _____   Last Name/Apellido Paterno _____

Account # with Company/# de Cuenta con la Compañía _____

Phone/Teléfono (_____)   Mobile Phone/Teléfono Celular (_____)

Email/Email _____

Street/Calle y Número _____   Apt #/Apto. _____

City/Ciudad _____   State/Estado _____   Zip/Código Postal _____

Amount
Certified
$

Fee
Cargo
$

Other Fee(s)
Otros Cargos
$

Tax
Impuesto
$

Total Amount Collected
Cantidad Total
= $

Exchange Rate
Tipo de Cambio

Amount to be Paid
Cantidad a Pagar

3 Consumer Signature

X _____

¹ IN ADDITION TO THE TRANSFER FEE, WESTERN UNION ALSO MAKES MONEY WHEN IT CHANGES YOUR DOLLARS INTO FOREIGN CURRENCY. PLEASE SEE ATTACHED PAGES FOR MORE INFORMATION REGARDING CURRENCY EXCHANGE. ◆ IF THE EXCHANGE RATE FOR YOUR TRANSACTION WAS DETERMINED AT THE TIME YOU SENT THE MONEY, THE CURRENCY TO BE PAID OUT AND THE EXCHANGE RATE ARE LISTED ON YOUR RECEIPT. OTHERWISE, THE EXCHANGE RATE WILL BE SET WHEN THE RECEIVER RECEIVES THE FUNDS. ◆ ¹ When sending $1,000 or more, the sender must provide identification and additional information. Dollar amount must not exceed US $5,000. ◆ Certain terms and conditions governing this transaction and the services you have selected are set forth on the attached pages. By signing this receipt, you are agreeing to those terms and conditions.

¹ ADEMÁS DEL CARGO POR EL ENVÍO, WESTERN UNION TAMBIÉN GANA DINERO CUANDO CAMBIA SUS DÓLARES A MONEDA EXTRANJERA. CONSULTE LOS DOCUMENTOS ANEXOS PARA OBTENER MÁS INFORMACIÓN SOBRE EL CAMBIO DE MONEDAS. ◆ CUANDO EL TIPO DE CAMBIO PARA LA TRANSACCIÓN SE HAYA FIJADO AL MOMENTO DE ENVIAR EL DINERO, LA MONEDA DE PAGO Y EL TIPO DE CAMBIO APLICADO SE INDICARÁN EN EL RECIBO DEL CLIENTE. EN CASO CONTRARIO, EL TIPO DE CAMBIO SE ESTABLECERÁ CUANDO EL DESTINATARIO COBRE EL DINERO. ◆ ¹ Para enviar una cantidad mayor o igual a $1,000, el remitente deberá proporcionar un documento de identidad y otros datos adicionales. El monto en dólares no debe exceder US $5,000. ◆ Algunos de los términos y condiciones que rigen la transacción y los servicios escogidos se establecen en los documentos anexos. La firma de este recibo es válida como expresión de consentimiento con tales términos y condiciones.

Date _____   Time _____   Agent's Signature _____

Here is a copy of the Wester Union form that I filled out to send payments to various creditors.

This is just one form of payment.

Appendix Page 18
Valid Settlement Letter

RE:
Account Number: **********
   Account Number:
Current Balance: $0.00
Paid: ($3,305.00)

Dear

This letter serves as confirmation that the above referenced account has been settled in full as of 08/31/2013.

This letter is contingent on the clearance of any check or ACH draft, and no charge back on any credit card payments made. If any check or ACH draft fails to clear, or there are any credit card charge backs, this letter is null and void.

Sincerely,

Collections Department

This is a valid, final settlement letter. Keep in a file forever, in case the creditor comes back wanting more money.

Appendix Page 19
Early on Correspondence from the Credit Card Companies

February 27, 2009

Account No.:

Dear

We understand that certain circumstances can affect people's ability to meet their financial obligations. To help you, we have many payment options. We can also put you in contact with a service that can work with your creditors to create a payment plan that is best for you. A financial management service can analyze your financial situation and work with your creditors to develop a monthly repayment plan that is best for you. There are several benefits you may receive by enrolling in a financial management program:

1. Allows you to consolidate your bills into one monthly payment.
2. Reduces your interest rates after your first payment is received.
3. We invite you to reapply for an account after you have successfully completed the program.
4. Helps you avoid further legal issues, such as bankruptcy.

If you have any questions, please call   Monday through Thursday from 8 a.m. to 10 p.m., Friday, 8 to 8, or Saturday, 9 to 2 (Eastern time). If you prefer, you may write to P.O. Box   Our knowledgeable Account Managers are ready to assist you.

Sincerely,

Customer Assistance department

P.S. For account information and payment options, visit us online at www.   com.

This is a letter from the credit card company early on. They were asking me to make arrangements with them. I had to wait a few more months before they would settle for a lower rate.

Appendix Page 20
Early on Correspondence from the Credit Card Companies

April 15, 2009

Account No

Dear

The above referenced account is currently past due. Many customers are struggling financially and   would like to make payment arrangements that will assist you.

Please call us today so that we can discuss the possibility of reducing your payment to $394 with a corresponding interest rate of 6%. Currently, this program is helping our customers make consistently lower monthly payments and paying off their debt.

You must call by April 28, 2009 to qualify for this offer

If you do not wish to take advantage of the above mentioned option, then the amount of $20,388 is due by April 28, 2009. Please call   Our knowledgeable Account Managers are ready to help you today.

Sincerely,

Customer Assistance Department

Call   **today!**
Monday through Thursday, 8 a.m. to 9 p.m.
Friday, 8 a.m. to 5 p.m.
Saturday, 8 a.m. to noon
Eastern time

Source Code:

This is a letter from the credit card company early on. They were asking me to make arrangements with them. I had to wait a few more months before they would settle for a lower rate.

Appendix Page 21
Early on Correspondence from the Credit Card Companies

May 2, 2009

Dear

Your credit card account is now scheduled to be written off as a bad debt next month.

Act Now – Or We'll Have to Write Off Your Account as a Bad Debt

Work with Us — Instead of a Collection Agency
Unless we receive a payment or you contact us by May 14, 2009, we may refer your account to a collection agency after it is written off.

Unfortunately, once that happens we will no longer be able to work with you and help you take the necessary steps to resolve your debt. In addition, for the next seven years any potential employer, mortgage company, car dealership, or creditor will be able to see this information on your credit file.

This means the time to act is now, and we have a special offer that can help.

We Can Help by Lowering Your Payments
If you call us today and make a payment of $490 by May 14, 2009, we'll lower your Annual Percentage Rate, which means your monthly payments will be lower. However, you must call the number below to be considered for this special offer.*

Please understand that by failing to make payment arrangements with us, we're forced to consider all our options. We're ready to work with you, so be sure to call us today.

Sincerely,

Customer Assistance Department

P.S. Remember – if you call us today you can avoid your account being written off as a bad debt and we can help you with your account by lowering your monthly payments.

Call today
Monday through Thursday, 8 a.m. to 8 p.m. Eastern time
Friday, 8 a.m. to 5 p.m. Eastern time Saturday, 8 a.m. to noon Eastern time
www. com

*Important information regarding this offer: You must call us to see if you are eligible and to receive additional information about this Program. At the end of the Program, or if during the Program your account becomes two billing cycles past due and a Minimum Payment has not been received within the past sixty (60) days, then on the first day of the next billing cycle, your account terms, for all new and existing balances, will return to the rates disclosed in your Credit Card Agreement, as may be amended. As required by this Program, you may not use the account until further notice.

This is a letter from the credit card company. They were asking me to make arrangements with them. I had to wait a few more months before I could save up the money.

76

Appendix Page 22
Early on Correspondence from the Credit Card Companies

May 04, 2009

Account No.:

Dear

The above-referenced account is several months past due. The account may be written off as a bad debt very soon. If the account is written off, we may refer the account to a collection agency and we will no longer be able to work with you at that time.

For the next seven years, any potential employer, mortgage company, car dealership, or creditor will be able to see this information on your credit file. To protect your credit rating, please pay $380.00 by May 15, 2009, or call our office to discuss a repayment plan.

If you are unable to make this payment, please call   Monday through Thursday from 8 a.m. to 9 p.m., Friday, 8 to 5, or Saturday, 8 to noon Eastern. Our knowledgeable associates can assist you with several available options.

Sincerely,

Customer Assistance Department

P.S. For account information and payment options, visit us online at www.   .com.

This is a letter from the credit card company early on. They were asking me to make arrangements with them. I had to wait a few more months before they would settle for a lower rate.

Appendix Page 23
Early on Correspondence from the Credit Card Companies

Don't miss this last chance to reduce your debt.

It's easy, convenient, and best of all – you'll save.

Call today to take advantage
of this special discount.

Monday through Friday, 8 a.m. to 8 p.m. EST
Saturday, 8 a.m. to noon EST

June 2, 2009

Dear

is giving you a unique opportunity to reduce your debt with this special offer.
Call us today to discuss payments toward this special final offer.

We're here to help.

We want to help you resolve your debt, which is why we are giving you this chance to settle your balance once and for all. **You can save 40% by settling your account. This is a savings of $8,231. To qualify for this offer you must call us at** to set **up payment arrangements on your account.**

Current Balance	Settlement Balance	You Save	That's a savings of 40%
$20,577	$11,852	$8,231	

Once you have paid your settlement balance, your debt will be resolved and your account will be closed.

Call us today to resolve your debt and save. If you don't contact us, your account may be referred to a third-party collections agency or an attorney for possible legal action, and your credit could be adversely affected.

Don't miss this great opportunity to save. **Call us today at**

Sincerely,

Customer Assistance Department

P.S. One call is all it takes to save. Pick up the phone today:

This is a letter from the credit card company. They were asking me to make arrangements with them. I had to wait a few more months before I could save up the money.

Appendix Page 24
Early on Correspondence from the Credit Card Companies

June 04, 2009

Account No.:

Dear

As you are aware, the above-referenced account is greater than 150 days past due and is scheduled to be written off as a bad debt on June 19, 2009. A payment of $320.00 will prevent this from happening.

You have been a customer since October 20, 1996, and we value your business. You have received several letters over the past six months offering various payment programs. We have also attempted to contact you by phone. We are concerned that we have not had the opportunity to offer you some alternatives to your account being written off as a bad debt. This will impact your credit history for the next seven years. When calling the number below, please ask for my extension,

Please call 1.800   Monday through Friday 8 a.m. - 9 p.m. or Saturday 8 a.m. - 12 p.m.. For account information and payment options, visit us online at www.   .com.

Sincerely,

Customer Assistance Department

This is a letter from the credit card company early on. They were asking me to make arrangements with them. I had to wait a few more months before they would settle for a lower rate.

Appendix Page 25
Valid Settlement Agreement

Wednesday, September 28, 2011

ACCOUNT IDENTIFICATION
Re

Account.   * * * * * * *

   Account No:
Balance: $1,077.57

Dear

This letter confirms that   duly authorized to accept $550.00 in Full Settlement of the above-referenced account. The settlement amount is due as follows.

Payment 01: $275.00   Due on: Friday, September 30, 2011

   Please secure your payment with a debit card or check by phone no later than: Wednesday, September 28, 2011 by 1:00pm EST.

Payment 02: $275.00   Due on: Sunday, October 30, 2011

Your payment must reach this office by the due date or this offer will become null and void. To ensure your funds are received by the due date,   accepts "Quick Check" by phone, Western Union "Quick Collect" (Code City:), Moneygram "Express Payment" (Receive Code: or you can make your payment online at www.   If your bank refuses to honor your check or other payment arrangements, this offer will become null and void.

Please do not respond to this email, if you have any questions, please contact your account representative at (800)   extension   Our office hours are Monday through Friday, 8:30am to 8:00pm, Pacific Time.

Sincerely,

Account Representative

THIS COMMUNICATION IS FROM A DEBT COLLECTOR. THIS IS AN ATTEMPT TO COLLECT A DEBT. ANY INFORMATION OBTAINED WILL BE USED FOR THAT PURPOSE.

NOTICE OF ELECTRONIC CHECK PROCESSING:

This is a valid settlement agreement, dated 09/28/11. Payments were made on time as requested, but I received a letter almost a year later saying I owed more money.

Appendix Page 26
Letter from Collection Agency

Phone:
Fax:

August 16, 2012

Principal Balance: $527.57
Interest Balance: $0.00
Balance Due: $527.57
Reference Number:
Account Number:

IMPORTANT SETTLEMENT OFFER

RE: Your Past Due Account With

We have previously notified you of the past due balance of $527.57 that has been placed with our office by

We have been authorized to accept a 55% settlement on this balance. This offer will be come null and void 30 days from the date of this letter. We are not obligated to renew this offer. If you would like to take advantage of this opportunity, please contact us today. Be advised that interest will continue to accrue until your payment is posted.

You may pay by check by phone now by calling our office toll-free at 888-   If you prefer to mail in your check, you may send it to:

Please call us with any questions or to verify your settlement amount.

This notice has been sent to you by a collection agency. This is an attempt to collect a debt; any information obtained will be used for that purpose.

Sincerely,

Unit Manager

Whenever $600.00 or more of a debt is forgiven as a result of settling a debt for less than the balance owing, the creditor may be required to report the amount of the debt forgiven to the Internal Revenue Service on a 1099C form, a copy of which would be mailed to you by the creditor. If you are uncertain of the legal or tax consequences, we encourage you to consult your legal or tax advisor.

Web pay available online at www.

PLEASE SEE REVERSE SIDE FOR IMPORTANT INFORMATION

* * * Detach Lower Portion and Return with Payment in the Enclosed Envelope * * *

Please make your checks payable to Citi.

CHANGE SERVICE REQUESTED

We accept VISA and MasterCard debit cards.
Please see reverse side for debit card payment.

August 16, 2012

This is the letter I received, almost a year later. So I had to send them a letter explaining that payments had been made according to the agreement and was satisfied.

Phone Number:
Principal Balance: $527.57
Balance: $0.00
                     $527.57
Reference Number:
Account Number:

Appendix Page 27
My Correspondence to the Collection Lawyer

8-31-2012

The following is in reference to Account #   , Ref.#   . Enclosed please find the letter that was sent to me by   and also the settlement letter, showing that a full settlement has been accepted by
Arrangements were made on Wednesday, Sept. 28, 2011 with
account representative   Full settlement agreement by both parties was made, agreeing, that there would be 2 payments: first on Friday Sept. 30, 2011, (check #   ) and the second on Sunday October 30, 2011, (check #   ). Both payments have been made, processed and cashed. Therefore, the agreement has been satisfied.

Any correspondence may be made to the above address until Oct. 1, 2012. After that date, any communication will need to go through my lawyer. He can be reached at the following address:

. Attention: Attorney

Here is a copy of the letter I sent by certified mail on 09/04/12. I have not heard from them since.

Appendix Page 28
Copies of 1099-C, Cancellation of Debt Forms

☐ CORRECTED (if checked)

CREDITOR'S name, street address, city, state, ZIP code, and telephone no.	1 Date canceled 12/31/2009	OMB No. 1545-1424	
Canceled Debt →	2 Amount of debt canceled $ 14487.44	**2009**	**Cancellation of Debt**
	3 Interest if included in box 2 $	Form **1099-C**	

CREDITOR'S federal identification number	DEBTOR'S identification number	4 Debt description VISA/MASTERCARD	**Copy B For Debtor**

DEBTOR'S name

This is important tax information and is being furnished to the Internal Revenue Service. If you are required to file a return, a negligence penalty or other sanction may be imposed on you if taxable income results from this transaction and the IRS determines that it has not been reported.

5 Was borrower personally liable for repayment of the debt?

[X] Yes ☐ No

Account number (see instructions)	6 Bankruptcy (if checked) ☐	7 Fair market value of property $

Form **1099-C**   (keep for your records)   Department of the Treasury - Internal Revenue Service

The amount of debt canceled is the amount that must be reported on the tax return.

***These 1099-Cs are from 2 different companies.**

COMBINED TAX STATEMENT FOR YEAR 2009

THIS STATEMENT REPORTS 1099-DIV (OMB No. 1545-0110), 1099-INT (OMB No. 1545-0112), 1099-OID (OMB No. 1545-0117), 1098 (OMB No. 1545-0901), 1099-MISC (OMB No. 1545-0115), 1099-B (OMB No. 1545-0715), 1099-Q (OMB No. 1545-1760), 1099-A (OMB No. 1545-0877), 1099-C (OMB No. 1545-1424), 1099-S (OMB No. 1545-0997), 1098-E (OMB No. 1545-1576), 1099-SA (OMB No. 1545-1517).
DEPARTMENT OF THE TREASURY-INTERNAL REVENUE SERVICE.

PAYERS E.I.N.

CUST SERV PH #

TAXPAYERS IDENTIFICATION NUMBER

"For Form 1099-B, DIV, INT, MISC, OID and Q: This is important tax information and is being furnished to the Internal Revenue Service. If you are required to file a return, a negligence penalty or other sanction may be imposed on you if this income is taxable and the IRS determines that it has not been reported."

ACCOUNT NUMBER	ACCOUNT TYPE	IRS DESCRIPTION	IRS BOX #	AMOUNT
	* * * 2009 FORM 1099-C, CANCELLATION OF DEBT * * *			
	BUSINESS CARD	AMT DEBT CANCELED	2 →	15196.08
	06/08/2009	DATE CANCELED	1	
SETTLEMENT DEFICIENCY BALANCE		DEBT DESCRIP	4	
	BORROWER WAS PERSONALLY LIABLE FOR REPAYMENT OF DEBT		5	

Canceled Debt

Appendix Page 29
Copies of 1099-C, Cancellation of Debt Forms

Tax Year 2009 Form 1099-C Cancellation of Debt (Copy B)

This is important tax information and is being furnished to the Internal Revenue Service. If you are required to file a return, a negligence penalty or other sanction may be imposed on you if taxable income results from this transaction and the IRS determines that it has not been reported.

Debtor's Information

Creditor's Information

Federal ID Number:

Form 1099-C Questions

Phone Support:

Debtor's ID Number:

Original

Summary of Form 1099-C Cancellation of Debt

(OMB No.

Box	Description	Amount	Box	Description	Amount
1.	Date Canceled	(See Details)	5.	Was borrower personally liable for repayment of the debt?	(See Details)
2.	Amount of debt canceled	$5,795.00	6.	Bankruptcy	No
3.	Interest if included in box 2	$0.00	7.	Fair market value of property	$0.00
4.	Debt Description	CREDIT CARD ACCOUNT			

Details of Form 1099-C Cancellation of Debt

(OMB No.

Account Number Acct Description	Box #1 Date canceled	Box #2 Amt. of debt canceled	Box #3 Int. included in box 2	Other Boxes	
	08/28/2009	$5,795.00	$0.00	#4 Debt description	CREDIT CARD ACCOUNT
				#5 Was borrower personally liable for repayment of the debt?	Yes
				#6 Bankruptcy	No

Canceled Debt

The amount of debt canceled is the amount that must be reported on the tax return.

Appendix Page 30
Copies of 1099-C, Cancellation of Debt Forms

Instructions for Debtor

Note. You may not have to include in income all or a portion of certain qualified principal residence indebtedness canceled in 2010. See Pub. 4681 for more information.

If a federal government agency, certain agencies connected with the Federal Government, financial institution, credit union, or an organization having a significant trade or business of lending money (such as a finance or credit card company) cancels or forgives a debt you owe of $600 or more, this form must be provided to you. Generally, if you are an individual, you must include all canceled amounts, even if less than $600, on the "Other income" line of Form 1040. If you are a corporation, partnership, or other entity, report the canceled debt on your tax return. See the tax return instructions.

However, some canceled debts are not includible, or fully includible, in your income, such as certain student loans, certain debts reduced by the seller after purchase, qualified farm debt, qualified real property business debt, qualified principal residence indebtedness, or debts canceled in bankruptcy. See Pub. 4681. Do not report a canceled debt as income if you did not deduct it but would have been able to do so on your tax return if you had paid it. Also, do not include canceled debts in your income to the extent you were insolvent immediately before the cancellation of the debt. If you exclude a canceled debt from your income, file Form 982.

Debtor's identification number. For your protection, this form may show only the last four digits of your social security number (SSN), individual taxpayer identification number (ITIN), or adoption taxpayer identification

number (ATIN). However, the issuer has reported your complete identification number to the IRS and, where applicable, to state and/or local governments.

Account number. May show an account or other unique number the creditor assigned to distinguish your account.

Box 1. Shows the date the debt was canceled.

Box 2. Shows the amount of debt canceled. **Note:** If you do not agree with this amount, contact your creditor.

Box 3. Shows interest if included in the canceled debt in box 2. See Pub. 525, to see if you must include the interest in gross income.

Box 4. Shows a description of the debt. If box 7 is completed, box 4 shows a description of the property.

Box 5. Shows whether borrower is personally liable for repayment of the debt. See Pub. 4681 for reporting instructions.

Box 6. If the box is marked, the creditor has indicated the debt was canceled in a bankruptcy proceeding.

Box 7. If, in the same calendar year, a foreclosure or abandonment of property occurred in connection with the cancellation of the debt, the fair market value (FMV) of the property will be shown, or you will receive a separate Form 1099-A. Generally, the gross foreclosure bid price is considered to be the FMV. For an abandonment or voluntary conveyance in lieu of foreclosure, the FMV is generally the appraised value of the property. You may have income or loss because of the acquisition or abandonment. If the property was your main home, see Pub. 523 to figure any taxable gain or ordinary income. See Pub. 4681 for information about foreclosures and abandonments.

☐ CORRECTED (if checked)

CREDITOR'S name, street address, city, state, ZIP code, and telephone no.	**1** Date canceled 7/10/2010	OMB No. 1545-1424 **2010**	**Cancellation of Debt**
Canceled Debt →	**2** Amount of debt canceled $ 9272.68		
	3 Interest if included in box 2 $	Form **1099-C**	
CREDITOR'S federal identification number	DEBTOR'S identification number	**4** Debt description Visa or Mastercard	**Copy B For Debtor**
DEBTOR'S name			This is important tax information and is being furnished to the Internal Revenue Service. If you are required to file a return, a negligence penalty or other sanction may be imposed on you if taxable income results from this transaction and the IRS determines that it has not been reported.
Street address (including apt. no.)		**5** Was borrower personally liable for repayment of the debt? ☒ Yes ☐ No	
City, state, and ZIP code			
Account number (see instructions)		**6** Bankruptcy (if checked) ☐	**7** Fair market value of property $	

Form **1099-C** (keep for your records) Department of the Treasury - Internal Revenue Service

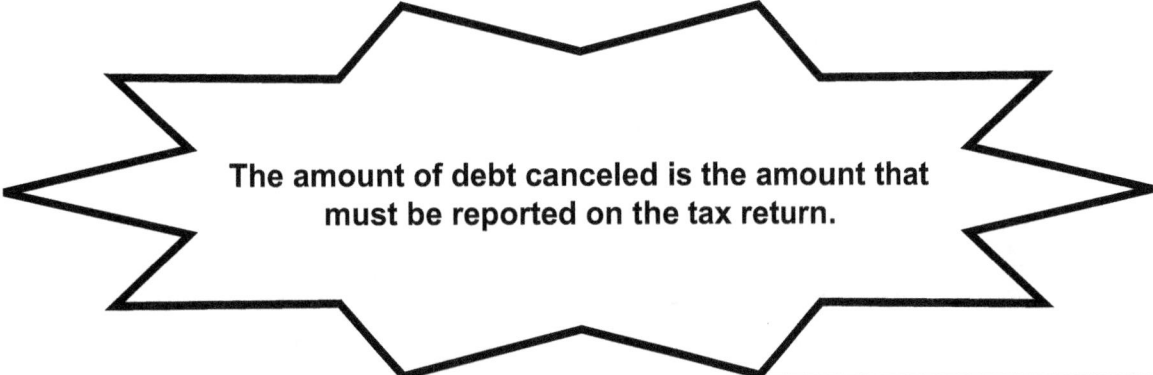

The amount of debt canceled is the amount that must be reported on the tax return.

Appendix Page 31
Copies of 1099-C, Cancellation of Debt Forms

Tax Year 2010 Form 1099-C Cancellation of Debt (Copy B)

This is important tax information and is being furnished to the Internal Revenue Service. If you are required to file a return, a negligence penalty or other sanction may be imposed on you if taxable income results from this transaction and the IRS determines that it has not been reported.

Debtor's Information

Creditor's Information

Federal ID Number:

Form 1099-C Questions

Phone Support:

Debtor's ID Number: **Original**

Summary of Form 1099-C Cancellation of Debt   (OMB No.

Box	Description	Amount	Box	Description	Amount
1.	Date Canceled	(See Details)	5.	Was borrower personally liable for repayment of the debt?	(See Details)
2.	Amount of debt canceled	$18,954.15	6.	Bankruptcy	No
3.	Interest if included in box 2	$0.00	7.	Fair market value of property	$0.00
4.	Debt Description	CREDIT CARD ACCOUNT			

Details of Form 1099-C Cancellation of Debt   (OMB No.   )

Account Number Acct Description	Box #1 Date canceled	Box #2 Amt. of debt canceled	Box #3 Int. included in box 2	Other Boxes	
	02/24/2010	$18,954.15	$0.00	#4 Debt description	CREDIT CARD ACCOUNT
				#5 Was borrower personally liable for repayment of the debt?	Yes
				#6 Bankruptcy	No

Canceled Debt

The amount of debt canceled is the amount that must be reported on the tax return.

Appendix Page 32
5th Party Letter

Statement Date:	08/31/16
ID Number:	
Original Creditor:	CAPITAL ONE
Current Creditor:	
Account Number:	XXXXXXXXXXXX
Total Current Balance:	$2,898.83

Your past due account(s) have been referred to our agency for collection. If you wish to resolve your obligation, call us toll free at
All payments must come to our office to ensure proper credit to your account.

This communication is from a debt collector. This is an attempt to collect a debt. Any information obtained will be used for that purpose. Unless you notify this office within 30 days after receiving this notice that you dispute the validity of the debt or any portion thereof, this office will assume this debt is valid. If you notify this office in writing within 30 days from receiving this notice, that the debt or any portion thereof is disputed, this office will obtain verification of the debt or obtain a copy of a judgment and mail a copy of such judgment or verification. If you request this office in writing within 30 days after receiving this notice, this office will provide you with the name and address of the original creditor, if different from current creditor.

Sincerely,

The law limits how long you can be sued on a debt. Because of the age of your debt   will not sue you for it and   will not report it to any credit reporting agency. If you make a partial payment on this account it may restart the statute of limitations on this account.

Here is a copy of a letter I received from a fifth party, trying to collect on a debt. I found it interesting that they admitted saying "the law limits how long you can be sued on a debt. Because of the age of your debt, ... will not sue you for it and ...... will not report it to any credit reporting agency."

But they still tried to get money from me. I sent them a letter explaining the Indiana law of legal theory called "accord and satisfaction." (See Appendix 13). I told them the debt was paid and told them if they had any questions that they could contact my lawyer. I never heard from them again.

Negotiating with Creditors

Be sure to take very detailed notes.
These charts are only a simple idea. You may want to modify them to fit your situation the best.

Creditor	Account Number	Contact Person	Phone # / Ext.

Balance Due	Terms / Payments	Settlement Date

Detailed Notes: <u>Date:</u> _____

_____

_____

_____

_____

_____

_____

_____

_____

_____

_____

_____

_____

_____

<u>Action to be taken:</u> _____

_____

_____

_____

_____

_____

It is ok to reproduce this page.

A Final Thought

Once again, I want to thank you for buying this book. As this book is going to print, there is a huge change in the economy. Millions of people are losing their job due to the coronavirus. Many of these people will be wondering how to make ends meet with little income. If you know somebody that is struggling, be sure to share this book with them. Also, if you could go to Amazon, Kindle, and our website www.findingfreedomfromdebt.com and give me a positive review, that would be highly appreciated. I want as many people to find encouragement through this book as possible. I have committed to give 50% of the profits from the sale of this book to non-profit organizations which includes, but not limited to, Samaritan's Purse International and U.S. Relief, World Missionary Press, Studio TEN Ministries, Focus on the Family, Compassion International, and more. Your purchase will touch lives throughout the world. Thank you.